PRAISE FOR THE SPIRITUALITY OF AWE

Schneider has produced a... work of passion, insight, advocacy, and public vision on perhaps the most important social topic of our time. Furthermore, it comes in a very readable package of short, digestible chapters, ideally suited for discussion in classrooms, book groups, and other platforms of learning. Like the work of our best public intellectuals, it is a scholarly treatise in which the scholarship supports the message without interfering with or obscuring the topic at hand.

~ Daniel Leichty, PhD, *Journal of Sociology and Social Welfare*

Kirk Schneider has done it again. One of the leading exponents of the existential/humanistic approach to daily living as well as to psychotherapy, Schneider brings a unique perspective to the study of robotics and artificial intelligence. Instead of claiming that these new technologies pose a threat to humanity, or that they represent an inevitable future to which humans must adjust, Schneider counsels that these challenges be faced with "adventure and awe." Instead of succumbing to the lure of a "transhuman" era, Schneider insists that it is technological advances that evoke what makes our species "truly human." In true existential/humanistic fashion, Schneider urges his readers to embrace what may seem to be "irrational" in the world [of the programmatic]. This is reminiscent of his previous writings on the "paradoxical mind," and how "cross-cultural spirituality" has coped with what seems to be a split between the rational and irrational aspects of humans and their world. Schneider has a fine grasp of the pertinent literature and his citations of contemporary research add substance to what could have been a simplistic polemic. Existential thought emphasizes choice while humanistic thought focuses on experience; Schneider combines both in a book that could not have been published at a more appropriate time. It deserves to be widely read, debated, discussed. and applied.

~Stanley Krippner, PhD, Consciousness Researcher, Professor Emeritus, Saybrook University, co-author of *Personal Mythology*

To Ellie,
May awe ligh

D0916423

11 Sept 2019

Kirk Schneider's [*The Spirituality of Awe* is a] provocative exploration of the dangers we face in an increasingly mechanized world.... Although clearly a...warning of serious moral, spiritual, and social danger, the book does not simply content itself with identifying problems and hand-wringing. Schneider provides a number of urgent recommendations for responding thoughtfully and forcefully to the robotic revolution in ways that seek to maintain our humanity, our agency, and sense of spiritual awe in the face of ever-growing threats from reductionist science, consumerism, and materialist social philosophies.

~ Edwin Gant, *Journal of Theoretical and Philosophical Psychology*

This slender volume is a manifesto...spurring us to preserve life-affirming and humanistic/existential values and practices in the era of Robotics.... For this reader the real value of Schneider's book...is in reminding us that the trans-human telos of technology is not inevitable. He reminds us that practicing the basic principles of phenomenology, taking time, paying attention...retaining a sense of the vast scale of our un-knowing and mastering the fear of our ignorance, will serve us well to guide our way to a future that is humane and not simply, post-human."

~ Richard Swann, *Existential Analysis: Journal of the Society for Existential Analysis*

The Spirituality of awe is a new take on the 'remorselessness of technology encroaching on our most intimate spaces.' It is a fast paced, easy-read dash through our technological future with the impending dangers of transhumanism at its core. In the end, as we enter the age of robotics, we are given the human choice to decide if we want an awe-inspiring dawn or a dehumanizing nightmare. Buy it. Read it. It is original."

~ Noel Sharkey, PhD, DSc, Emeritus Professor of AI and Robotics, Sheffield University, UK, Judge BBC television's *Robot Wars* and Director of the Foundation for Responsible Robotics

Schneider's 'depth psychology' approach casts new light on a classic dilemma in AI's inevitable march—bringing us all the promise and peril that science fiction writers have warned about for centuries.

~ Mike Boland, Chief Analyst, ARtilliry, former reporter, Forbes

The dehumanization of life in the new computer driven society leads to a gradual death of feeling. When people are cut off from feeling they are more likely to act out in destructive and potentially violent behavior.... In this important book, the author offers an alternative in his conception of an awe-based psychology that emphasizes both the mystery and magnificence of existence. I am personally inspired by Schneider's ethical approach to coping with the problem of maintaining one's human heritage in the new society.

~ Robert Firestone, PhD, author of *Overcoming the Destructive Inner Voice: True Stories of Therapy and Transformation,* and (with Joyce Catlett) *Beyond Death Anxiety: Achieving Life-affirming Death Awareness*

In a world where many feel dehumanized and devalued, we need courage and clarity to widen our perspective and find new purpose. In this book Kirk Schneider offers a sensitive and incisive new narrative to help us reconsider what our lives are about today. He gathers wisdom from his long experience, and freely combines this with the insights of psychology, psychotherapy, philosophy, sociology, religion, literature and cinema to create a new vision of where we are heading and how we may change direction before it is too late. Fascinating and essential reading for therapists and lay readers alike.

~ Prof Emmy van Deurzen, PhD, Principal of the New School for Psychotherapy and Counseling, UK; author of *Existential Psychotherapy and Counselling in Practice* and *Psychotherapy and the Quest for Happiness.*

An evocative and deeply human take on the coming AI and robotics age. You must read it.

~Gina Smith, PhD, Award-winning author of *The Genomics Age* and the NYT bestseller, *iWOZ: How I Invented the Personal Computer*

A cogent plea to neither reject nor embrace technology, but to try instead to look beyond it.

~ *Kirkus Reviews*, Featured Review

The Spirituality of Awe clearly brings to light deep concerns, positive or negative, many people share living in this age of robotic revolution. [This] revolution has brought about the ideology of transhumanism which blurs the human-machine divide. From the viewpoint of depth and existential psychology, the author counters it with neo-humanism. While admitting the seemingly extraordinary benefit of convenience and widening capacity to live, he asks what may have already been, is now and will be further lost by the uncritical dependence on products from the revolution. It is the core of humanity: adventure and awe without which one's identity and dignity as a human being would be seriously threatened. Relying in part on his personal experiences, he concretely explores, without denying high technology altogether, an awe-inspired way of life.

~ Shoji Muramoto, PhD, Professor emeritus, Kobe City University of Foreign Studies, Japan, former editor-in-chief of the *Japanese Journal of Humanistic Psychology*, author of Buddhist and Jungian studies

The question of how we live is increasingly crucial in this age of technology, high-tech devices and robotics. In this timely and inspiring book, Dr. Schneider offers a fascinating and comprehensive analysis of the unique challenges and concerns of humanity in the face of such a reality. He perceptively and sensitively touches on enduring qualities that are at the core of our existence as human beings – spirituality, vulnerability, wonder, imagination, love, creativity and discovery – and identifies them as the delicate ingredients that have the potential to reconnect us with the beautiful, mysterious and awe-inspiring experience of being fully and meaningfully alive.

~ Pninit Russo-Netzer, PhD, Lecturer and Researcher, University of Haifa; co-editor of *Meaning in Positive and Existential Psychology* and *Clinical Perspectives on Meaning: Positive and Existential Psychotherapy*

The Spirituality of Awe: Challenges to the Robotic Revolution

By Kirk J. Schneider, PhD

University
PROFESSORS PRESS
www.universityprofessorspress.com

Revised edition first published in 2019. University Professors Press. Colorado
Springs, CO, United States.

ISBN 13: 978-1-939686-27-5
ISBN 10: 1-939686-27-X

University Professors Press
Colorado Springs, CO
www.universityprofessorspress.com

Cover Image by Bob Eggleton
Original Cover Design by Thomas Ewing of aNewDomain
Cover Design adapted by Laura Ross

*First edition published by Waterfront Press. Revised edition published with
permission.*

There's a time when the operation of the machine becomes so odious, makes you so sick at heart, that you can't take part! You can't even passively take part! And you've got to put your bodies upon the gears and upon the wheels...upon the levers, upon all the apparatus, and you've got to make it stop! And you've got to indicate to the people who run it, to the people who own it, that unless you're free, the machine will be prevented from working at all!
~ Mario Savio, student activist, U.C. Berkeley, 1964

Mystery, as it was known in primordial rite and ritual, as it was experienced in the sacraments of the mystery cults, had stood as a boundary defining [humanity's] proper station in the world....it served to enrich [people] by confronting them with a realm of inexhaustible wonder! With the appearance of scientific skepticism, however, the mysterious either became a tricky puzzle to be solved or a guilty secret to be exposed. In either case, mystery came to be seen as an intolerable barrier to reason and justice. Since the sacred had become the mask of scoundrels and fiends, away then with the sacred!
~ Theodore Roszak, *The Making of a Counter Culture*

As I reflect on the matter...I do remember moments when I have been awe awakened; there have been times that I have been carried out of myself by something greater than myself and to that something I gave myself.
~ Martin Luther King, *The Autobiography of Martin Luther King*

Table of Contents

Preface to the Revised Edition[1]

The urgency of this book has grown. As people scramble for quick fixes and instant results, the gap between the spirituality of awe and the machine model for living is an ever-widening morass. People have a hard time being curious and respectful these days, let alone talking to one other. We're hardening hearts and hardening minds, just like our hardware; lashing out and lashing back, reflexively kicking and kicking back. Furthermore, we're being increasingly controlled by our "primitive" brains, our hormones and our serotonin, our dopamine and our drugs—everything it seems but our whole body experience and the bigger picture of life. This picture is diverse, extensive, humbling and grand, and it demands sustained discernment. Yet the split between those who foster awe—humility and wonder, sense of adventure toward living, and those who foment polarization—imperiousness, rigidity, and single points of view is grave; and as the world swells with stereotypes, sloganeering, and knee-jerk animosities, the military-industrial technocracy grows in proportion.

It is now no longer a quesiton of whether the expansion of consciousness is "desirable," it is imperative. If there is one lesson to be learned over the past year it is how susceptible we *all* are to digitally driven, ideologically based propaganda. Whomever the powers that be, be they countries, leaders, corporations, or crooks, whomever has their clutches on the techno-industrial levers, has a vast capacity to kill—and I'm talking about killing spirits here as much as human lives. What we have learned from facebook and snapchat and twitter feeds and infotainment of all sorts is how easily many of us go into "robotic" mode. This is a mode of elemental reactions, narrowed perceptions, and rigidified assumptions about the world. Sometimes we are lured but mainly we are spooked into these abrupt new forms of ourselves. We

---

[1] For this book, the author and publisher elected not to follow the APA style formatting. Reference information is provided in footnotes.

then go about the world doing the bidding of others—even if we vaguely realize, and resent, that we are doing their bidding. This is because, eventually, as we are surrounded by enough gimmickry, we have a reduced consciousness of what we are doing or who we are serving. We now know more about how roboticism—the machine model for living—can induce us into a kind of stupor. This stupor incites us to buy things we don't need, vote for platforms or candidates who oppose our interests, and believe we are our own agents when we have nonconsciously forfeited that agency to others.

What all this amounts to is the erosion of choice—and the erosion of choice is the surest road to autocracy; the collapse of democracy. Now more than ever I am convinced that "the better angels of our nature," as Lincoln once put it, have little chance to emerge without reinstilling the awe for life—without stemming roboticism, without curbing the quick-fix, instant results world capped off by militarism and the surveillance state.

While some have criticized the realistic nature of this awe-based stance, I question whether they are thinking in the strategic manner that I have set forth in this book. Despite more than a few passages that are aspirational, even romantic in nature, I have conspicuously included concrete suggestions about how we can implement awe-based child-rearing, education, work environments, religious and spiritual settings, and governmental relations. I have also concertedly discussed actual programs that bring people together for face-to-face dialogues, as distinct from encounters over social media or cable news, to discover who their fellow human beings are as multifaceted *persons*.

In this context, I have joined a new organization over this past year, aptly named "Better Angels" (https://www.better-angels.org), which fosters such awe-based collectivism on an unprecedented scale. Better Angles is a grass roots society that promotes highly structured, psychologically supportive dialogues between liberals and conservatives throughout the U.S. The mission of Better Angels is for each "side" to understand and learn from one another, not to persuade, impose or cajole; and their emphases on "respect," "curiosity," and "openness" are very close to the awe-based stances of the dialogue groups that I describe in chapter 6 of this book. The emerging outcomes of Better Angels' gatherings are also resonant with those I describe in chapter 6, and as I believe many would agree, this is a remarkably hopeful development, for us all.

The depth psychologists and philosophers throughout history have long centered on the holding of paradox as key to our invidual and collective well-being. We might now say that the awe for life, for our smallness as well as greatness, our fragility as well as boldness is one of the deepest most enriching paradoxes that we can experience; it is also one of the most trying. Are we ready to grapple with such paradoxes in our everyday lives—within ourselves and among our fellow citizens? Are we ready to get out of our own way, humble ourselves to the point of discomfort and open ourselves to the point of intrigue or even amazement at what we may learn? Are we ready to really "hear" and enable the contrasting voices within and without, let them jostle and tumble about in order to—just possibly—find conciliation in those voices, a new synthesis that could expand and deepen our view? These are the seeds of what we need right now, the budding of a renewed or even better "deep" democracy that will counter the regimentation and leveling of life fostered by the machine model. Again, that model does not have to dehumanize, it can facilitate our awe-based aims. But we have to be wary toward it—to ask direct questions, such as does this device I now hold in my hands foster or repel my (and our) quest to live meaningfully, poignantly, as if every moment mattered. These are the questions that I have grappled with in this book—and that still bear heavily on my being.

Kirk Schneider
January, 2019

Prologue:
The Slippery Slope of Robotics

Virtually every social peril we face today is traceable to roboticism; our tendency to act like and be replaced by machines. As I write these words, we're in the midst of a firestorm of twitter feeds, fictional news stories and unfiltered propaganda that all seem to converge on one basic purpose: to compel a needy populace to "heel" at the foot of the powerful. Right here in the freedom-loving U.S.A., we have been thrust into a fantasy world of strong-arm leadership, simplistic sloganeering and monarch-style nationalism. It's not that these qualities have been absent at earlier times in history; far from it. But now they are showing up in ways, both subtle and gross, that permeate civic life.

Are we truly entering the age of the Orwellian nightmare with the control of large swaths of the U.S. population, whether by gun or computer or ideology, desperate to be controlled? Desperate to be lifted out of their own nightmare of physical and emotional impoverishment, the grind of routine, the hollowness of relationship, whether corporate or domestic or communal?

Just where is the world of texting and Instagram and Snapchat, automated news, communication through sound bytes, religion "to go" and endless streaming taking us? How has it made us susceptible to a government that mocks freedom of the press, squelches inquiry and chides the dialogues among nations, ethnicities and cultures? Is it any wonder that some 60 million of us in the United States have chosen this contraction, just as the speed, instant results and packaging of technology have reached an historical peak? We're looking for FIXES in part because this is what our age promises, and on the other hand, provides little or no help to counter.

Automation, the machine-model for living, is permeating our consciousness (as well as our work force!) and many of us welcome it, indeed hunger for it on a myriad of levels. This problem is no less true in many other parts of the world, particularly militarily.

Yet what is lost in this headlong embrace is depth[2]; the awe-

---

[2] By "depth" I mean an attunement to one's whole-bodied experience of life, and in particular, subconscious and meta-conscious life as explained later in the book.

someness, not just of our machines, but of our flesh, our capacity to feel, and our capacity to dwell in the miracle of the unknown.

Does our technology enhance this venture, divert us from it, point us toward it? Probably all three. But why aren't we using our newfangled gadgets to tap into every corner of our aliveness and our abilities to foster aliveness in others? Why is it mostly such a grind for people, and the nagging sense that we are marching collectively—and willingly!—to our doom. This at least is what many of our science fiction writers warn. Our artists. But it is also what I see daily as a depth psychotherapist[3]—the shaken spirits of once animated souls; abysses of pain in the heart of silicon glitter.

The outlook, moreover, is no less concerning. For today we face not just automated "enhancements," but literal "replicants." These are creations that may not just substitute for, but could potentially replace our mortal coils.

Such are a few of the heavy, and indeed central questions that I pursue in this volume. I do all I can not to lapse into either nay-saying cynicism or bright-eyed enthusiasm—but rather to shoot straight from the heart. As a depth psychologist, and as a privileged witness to people's most intimate stories (including my own), I try to tell it plain about what it's like to live here, now in this harrowing new age. I feel it's my duty.

Kirk J. Schneider
March, 2017

---

[3] As a depth psychotherapist, my emphasis is on longer-term, relational encounter. I also focus on complex life issues, such as freedom, finitude, and meaning, and not merely outward behaviors.

Introduction:
The Rise of Transhumanism

The question facing us is not 'How shall we know?'
but 'How shall we live?'
~Theodore Roszak,
The Making of a Counter-Culture

The robotic revolution is here. Everything from monarchies to autocracies to advertising has paved the way for it—but now there is a movement that is about to "put the icing on the cake," and the very definition of being human will be at stake. Indeed, the very definition of being an autonomous, mortal animal will be at stake, and there will be no going back. The movement to which I refer is "transhumanism," sometimes also called "posthumanism." Transhumanism advocates nanotechnology, genetic engineering and robotics to radically transform consciousness. [1] It is both a national and international movement and it is about to steamroll our world.

This book, accordingly, is about our growing capacity to play God. As a humanist and spiritual inquirer, this capacity both frightens and intrigues me.

Yet this book is not mainly about me, but about *us*. Its main focus is on the kind of society we would like to see evolve, the urgency of that quest, and the steps it will take to achieve it. As implied by the title of this book, *The Spirituality of Awe*, I believe that in spite of and even in light of the robotic revolution, life can be both humbling and grand; poignant and adventurous.[2] It can be *awesome*. But the first step toward

---

[1] The definition of transhumanism was drawn from Wikipedia—retrieved 12/26/16 from https://en.wikipedia.org/wiki/Transhumanism, as well as Ray Kurzweil's *The Singularity is Near* (New York: Viking, 2006). Further, transhumanism can be seen as one branch of "posthumanism," which is a more general term that investigates the changing definition of a human being in a techno-scientific world (see https://en.wikipedia.org/wiki/Posthumanism retrieved 12/26/16).

[2] For an elaboration on how "life can be both humbling and grand, poignant and adventurous" or in short "awe-filled," see Kirk Schneider *Rediscovery of Awe: Splendor, Mystery, and the Fluid Center of Life* (St. Paul, MN: Paragon House, 2004) as well as

attaining such a life is to pause, collect our breaths and see what we've been granted; and the second step is to realize that struggle, *some form of human vulnerability,* will inevitably attend.

I write this book in the midst of struggle. I have a neurological condition called cervical dystonia, which affects a very small percentage of the population. Cervical dystonia causes an involuntary turning of the neck, and if I didn't use an array of exercises, low dose medications and botox injections directly into my neck, my head would probably "lock" to the side. I am greatly challenged by this condition, particularly when I walk and socialize. At the same time, due to many factors—not least of which has been my background as both psychotherapist and incredibly grateful recipient of psychotherapy—I have made notable progress in addressing my condition. I am also challenged by several other blows I've received over my six decades—from the death of my seven-year-old brother when I was two to the fatal heart attacks of my father, uncle and grandfather by their early 50s.

That said, and what I mainly want to get across is that we're ALL struggling in some form. We've all had major and minor blows; the question is how are we handling them, and how *will* we handle them in the face of mounting biotechnical reform?

However, one stands on this admittedly thorny issue, I contend that, despite their costs, some level of anxiety, vulnerability—appreciation for *mystery*—are absolutely imperative if we as a species are to thrive. And if we become deaf to this proposition, we will lose the best of who we are and can become.

This book then is a will and testament of sorts—though hopefully not my last!—on the awe-inspired life; not as an all-pervading Answer, but as a desperately fading complement to a frightfully exhilarating revolution just upon our horizon. That revolution, as the futurist Ray Kurzweil and others have called it, is transhumanism.

One final point: Although there have been mounting critiques of the robotic revolution—see the superb reflections by Sherry Turkle, Yoseph Bar Cohen and David Hanson, and even Stephen Hawking[3]—

Awakening to awe: Personal stories of profound transformation (Lanham, MD: Jason Aronson).

[3] For elaborations, see the incisive critiques of the robotic revolution in Sherry Turkle's *Reclaiming Conversation: The Power of Talk in a Digital Age* (New York: Penguin, 2015), Yoseph Bar Cohen and David Hanson's *The Coming Robot Revolution: Expectations and Fears About Emerging Intelligent, Humanlike Machines* (New York: Springer, 2009) and Adam Alter's *Irresistible: The Rise of Addictive Technology and the Business of Keeping Us Hooked* (New York: Penguin, 2017). Note also the chilling words of astrophysicist

most of these focus on its *symptoms* and not the dynamics that drive those symptoms. For example, there are many studies about how computerization is shortening attention spans, creating internet addicted youth and cutting back on in-depth communications. There are also numerous studies on technology and class divisions, levels of education and adversaries at war. However, there have been relatively few studies looking at the underlying dynamics of those problems, and particularly from the standpoint of depth-psychological reform. This book, accordingly, is one attempt to bridge the gap, to examine the impact of robotics on human beings' *inner* as well as outer worlds, and to consider how best to invigorate those worlds.

Stephen Hawking who stated on the British Broadcasting Corporation that "the development of artificial intelligence could spell the end of mankind," and further added: "humans who are limited by slow biological evolution couldn't compete and would be superseded." Retrieved 12/26/16 from http://www.bbc.com/news/technology-30290540

Chapter 1

Keeping the Human in the New Human

High tech fulfills many needs; most of them physical, informational and commercial. What it tends not to fulfill are "existential needs"—purpose, connection, awe for life.

> ~ Paraphrased from a discussion with friend and colleague, Kathleen Galvin, PhD

Daily experience has been reduced to the size of four-inch screens while a simple tilt of the head toward the cosmos would reveal 'the greatest show on earth.'

> ~ Jeff Schneider, personal communication, February 13, 2017

I lose my smart phone and feel like a piece of myself is missing. I go about the house searching for it and think "what am I searching for?" I'm one of the *least* users of this technology. I usually keep my phone off, for example, to limit its electromagnetic fields. I check my phone perhaps every other day, and I am reluctant, on principle, to text, so that I can avoid the obsessiveness that seems inexorably to accompany it. And yet here I am feeling less than whole because I'm missing my phone!

What seems increasingly clear to me (and researchers like Sherry Turkle[1]) is that like it or not, technology is encroaching on how we see the world. Or to put it another way, we're becoming "internalized machines." Even though I'm a very limited user, just knowing that I have a quick and easy way to call my wife, or check an email, or use a GPS system, is acutely comforting. Whereas without those conveniences, I

---

[1] For an elaboration on how technology shapes our responses to the world, see Sherry Turkle's "The Empathy Gap: Digital Culture Needs What Talk Therapy Offers." *Psychotherapy Networker*, November/December, 2016, 29-55.

feel a little lost. Moreover, if you think such contrivances have horse-collared me, just think what the typical 12-year-old experiences when she misplaces *her* phone—all-out panic!

Extrapolate these issues to our everyday worlds, and we see that many people quite literally are enslaved to their devices; and the result of such enslavement is an atrophied capacity to live without them. We see such syndromes in the streets, in cars and in homes. We also assuredly see them in schools, in workplaces, and increasingly, even at resorts! (There are few things more ironic than watching scores of sun worshipers fingering their iPads!).

It's not that all these preoccupations with devices are evil; they are the way of the world, the way of evolution, and a logical extension of our capacity to thrive. They are ingenious assistants in our navigations through business, education and play; and increasingly, they are critical to our physical and at times, emotional health. The computer on which I type these words for example is far more pleasurable to write on than the old hunt-and-peck method procured for my electric typewriter. I can enjoy the flow of ideas as they briskly move from brain to electronic print, and from electronic print to my laser printer.

At the same time, there is a cost to this wizardry, and it has barely begun to emerge; at least not in proportion to its threat. And what is that threat? For one, it is way beyond the usual drumbeats in the media about the "health effects" of cell phones and video games. It is far beyond the effects of these devices on our personalities or interactions with friends.

There is something much larger at stake here, and we must not be naïve about it. What we have on our hands and what is about to explode in our bodies and brains! is nothing less than that "transhumanist" revolution to which I alluded earlier. By transhumanist, again, I take my cue from futurists like Ray Kurzweil who advocate for the transformation of human beings into something radically different from our pretechnological state. They advocate for a transformation that is poised to thoroughly redefine who and what we are, and that increasingly blurs the human-machine divide. It even blurs the human-cosmos divide to the point seemingly where it will be humans and not "acts of nature" who determine the fate of existence.

Kurzweil, a Stanford professor and Google engineer, puts it boldly:

> There is now a grand project underway involving many thousands of scientists and engineers working to understand

the best example we have of an intelligent process: the human brain....The goal of the project is to understand precisely how the human brain works, and then to use these revealed methods to better understand ourselves, to fix the brain when needed, and ... to create even more intelligent machines.[2]

Not one to be content with merely human changes, Kurzweil notes that our ultimate task is to "[wake] up the universe, and then intelligently [decide] its fate by infusing it with our human intelligence in its nonbiological forms." This is "our destiny."[3]

Finally, in Kurzweil's *How to Create a Mind: The Secret of Human Thought Revealed*, he references fellow theorist Steven Harnad's view: "If a machine can prove indistinguishable from a human, we should award it the respect we would to a human—we should accept that it has a mind."[4]

To put it baldly, the transhumanist revolution is breaking into everything from designer drugs to virtual reality simulators to neural implants, and from omni-surveillance to mechanized body parts—with the ultimate goal of a crime-free, disease-free, and anxiety-free existence, in which one merely needs to "plug in" to function optimally. Just consider the oft' reported wish list of transhumanist "benefits:"

Short-range Vision (partially presently achieved):
- Algorithmically-driven advertising, medicine, psychotherapy and ethics. For example, we now have legions of apps to "treat" anxiety and depression. They are being sold by the thousands.
- Miniaturized operating systems capable of interacting with their users and accessing the world-wide web. Such operating systems can be worn, for example, as earbuds depicted in the film *Her.*
- Designer babies, or genetically engineered and "optimized" kids.
- Designer drugs—such as "memory erasers," and drug– induced eradication of most major natural diseases.

---

[2] "There is now a grand project underway..." is from Ray Kurzweil's *How to Create a Mind: The Secret of Human Thought Revealed* (New York: Penguin, 2013, p. 5).

[3] "[wake] up the universe..." is from Ray Kurzweil's *How to Create a Mind: The Secret of Human Thought Revealed* (New York: Penguin, 2013, p. 282).

[4] Kurzweil's quote of Steven Harnad is on p. 266 from *How to Create a Mind.*

- The development of artificial intelligence, guiding our lives through computerization, transportation and robotic assistance.
- Robot-authored news, blogs and even "creative" fiction.

Long-range Vision:
- The transcendence of suffering and death through cybernetic (computerized) technology.
- The replacement of neural networks with silicon chips which can replicate brain functioning.
- The replacement of natural intelligence with artificial, computerized intelligence.
- The replacement of "defective" body parts through cybernetic technology.
- Self-replicating "nanobots" capable of replicating inexhaustible generations of both tools and weaponry.
- The achievement of a "singularity," where robotics may completely replace human administration and industry, and where humans, as such, become decreasingly relevant. This "achievement" moreover threatens to entirely decenter the self and is eerily reminiscent of some New Age and postmodern views of consciousness. Who or what is in control at this stage of being, and how susceptible is it to corporate and political manipulation?
- Finally, here's how Kurzweil summarized the future at a 2013 conference:

We're going to become increasingly non-biological to the point where the non-biological part dominates and the biological part is not important any more. In fact the non-biological part—the machine part—will be so powerful it can completely model and understand the biological part. So even if that biological part went away it wouldn't make any difference.

Kurzweil goes on:

We'll also have non-biological bodies—we can create bodies with nanotechnology, we can create virtual bodies and virtual reality in which the virtual reality will be as realistic as the actual reality. The virtual bodies will be as detailed and convincing as real bodies.[5]

That said, no doubt that many transhumanist innovations would enhance human functioning. No doubt that they would expedite information, industrial production and well-being across wide swaths of our lives. Transhumanism might even overcome war and eventually human mortality. But at what cost, and is transhumanism the best route to achieve these aims? I contend in this book that we must very carefully weigh these questions and for one chief reason: the loss of "adventure and awe." By adventure and awe I mean the humility and wonder, or continual openness to discovery. This is an openness that leans on our vulnerability as well as our boldness and that is inexhaustible—virtually—in its illumination of existence. As we shall see, adventure and awe are key to the perpetuation of vibrant, evolving lives—and in combination with technological advances may bring marvels to our emerging repertoires. But in the absence of these aforementioned sensibilities, our technologies become dead ends; closures; prisons of efficiency. They become *expedient* and yet devoid of the MORE or mystery that ceaselessly allures.

The challenge here is to operate in and out of the machine. The machine (or device) is a closed system and closure limits awe. On the other hand, if we can be conscious of these closed systems, we can step out of the game and into the "open systems" of life, the intensities of life. For example, we can make raw contact with our bodies, with nature, and with our imaginations. Although these realms have organic limits, they are not subject to the calculative manipulations of machines. They leave us freer therefore but also more vulnerable; humbler yet bolder, which are precisely the earmarks of awe. The core question then is not whether we use our technologies, it's whether—*even during their use*—

---

[5] The quote "We're going to become increasingly non-biological..." and ending on p. 15 is from Kurzweil at the Global Futures 2045 International Congress, June, 2013. The quote is reported in "Google's Ray Kurzweil: 'Mind Upload,'" by John Thomas Didymus, *Digital Journal*, June 20, 2013. Retrieved 12/26/16 from http://www.digitaljournal.com/article/352787). I want to be clear that my concern with Kurzweil's work is not in it's laudable attempts to expand and shape our human destiny—this is a birthright of our capacity for freedom. However, my reservations are in the scientist's vision of how that destiny is to be expanded and shaped—to wit its technicism. See also Rollo May's trenchant observations on this matter in his *Freedom and Destiny* (New York: Norton, 1981) and Yuval Harari's *Homo Deus* (New York: Harper, 2017).

we can break out of the mindset that they promote.

On the pages to follow, I will elaborate on these potential breakthroughs as well as breakdowns. I will draw on my personal experiences as well as those of the collective at this critical juncture. But in order to clarify the context within which we presently find ourselves, we must first consider the history that has led up to it. In many ways, this is an underground history about which too few are aware; but many more should be if we are to come to grips with the forces which beset (and threaten) us, and that leave hints as to our renewal.

Chapter 2

With Both Eyes Open:
Facing the Frankensteinian Nightmare

To more fully understand the transhumanist threat, we need to look back at a critical juncture of our Western heritage. This juncture has only been hinted at in conventional texts, but is a subterranean milestone in the contemporary psyche of humanity.

On the cusp of the Renaissance, Western society took a breakneck turn. The leaders of the time surveyed the terrain of the last half millennium, also called the "Dark Ages," and were aghast at what they saw: a centuries-long crusade to rid the world of (non-Christian) infidels; 19,000 leprosy colonies in the heart of Europe; a "Black Death," otherwise known as the Bubonic plague, destroying roughly 25 million people; a frenzy of ethnic and religious slaughter, and a tidal wave of impoverishment and squalor.[1]

Consequently, some of these Renaissance leaders (and particularly their successors in the Enlightenment) flew into a frenzy of their own. Their new moniker was a "rebirth" of a Greco-Roman ideal—a new rationality, a fresh cause to rid the world of its diseases and corruption, to "clean," as it were the "filth" of the last half millennium and to base their cause on reason, industriousness and science. But along with these reformations came some menacing consequences.

According to historians such as Michel Foucault, key Renaissance leaders—and particularly those bent on industrialization—turned their backs on nature. And by spurning nature, they rejected linkages to mystery, the uncontained, and ultimately the spontaneous and spiritual. The consequence of this backlash—now termed "Rationalism,"—was an almost wholesale effort to sanitize life, both in mind and body. A chief, and for some, unintended outcome of this sanitization program was to prioritize that which was perceived as

---

[1] Material in this section is drawn from Michel Foucault's *Madness and Civilization* (New York: Vintage, 1961).

health, convenience and profit—largely for those fortunate enough to access such opportunities, namely middle to upper class white males. But the trend line was clear: it swung toward a world in which day-to-day life could be efficient, methodically ordered and technically advanced.

What then has become of such a world? Mary Shelley gave us hints of it with her 1818 classic *Frankenstein*. In this iconic tale, a traumatized scientist sets about to create an immortal being made of electricity and dead body parts. But he naively constructs a "monster" that destroys both itself and many with whom it comes into contact.

Will our world go the same route? This is what we must plumb carefully. While the Renaissance, roughly from the 14th to the 17th century, soared brilliantly in the lives of many—particularly in the realms of art and science, the general standard of living, and the reawakening of interest in *human* (as distinct from divine) potentiality—signs of menace were also already evident. This menace reflected a panic and a contempt that propelled the Renaissance legacy into its succeeding era of industrialization and the "Age of Enlightenment." What began as a transition toward rejuvenation, shifted subtly toward polarization: an increasing antipathy toward our primal past and an abrupt severance from our bewildering yet invigorating anxieties.

These anxieties were triggered first and foremost before the wilds of nature—sea, sky and forest. The sea, for example, became an increasing symbol of chaos which needed to be tamed and managed. Similarly, the mad or those who were considered "useless" from the standpoint of industrialized labor, were not only equated with the sea; they were driven into it. The so-called "Ship of Fools" became a literal and figurative symbol by which the mad could not only be segregated from civic life; but potentially "restored" by their restive relative— water. The outcome, however, was far from the alleged aspiration, as legions of innocent and formerly tolerated civilians were cast off and banished to their watery graves.

The sea also became a commercial lane for trade and conquest. Of course, there was still a romance to the sea, but increasingly, like so much in the industrialized world, it became an "instrument" of use for merchants and armies alike.

The sky too became a tool of sorts, yielding its bounty for smoke stacks and waste. And soon enough, the skies became the receptacles for commercial air traffic and military weaponry. How distant these developments became from their cathedral building, wondering and wandering forebears.

The forest too became a barrier to be cleared, cut and urbanized. The forest, or in its more primal form, jungle, also became a place of increasing menace—marked by darkness and filth. The jungle was for the "savage" or animalistic, not the gentlemanly or gentlewomanly civilian of the 17th through 21st centuries. Indeed, for many during these "enlightened" years, the people of the jungle were almost invariably perceived as dark, both physically and mentally—and the darker the scarier; the darker the more linked with disarray. Even prior to 1600, the color black was almost strictly associated with that which was dirty and foul; with the night and the unpredictable. By contrast, the color white was almost invariably associated with purity, cleanliness and modernity.[2]

What we see here is a Western world that plunged headlong into a linear, rationalistic and mechanized value system. This was a world that clamped down on spontaneity, deviation from the norm and craft, and contrastingly flung the gates open to regimentation and control. Here's how Foucault put it in his inimitable style:

> let us [consider]...madness as the manifestation in man [woman] of an obscure and aquatic element, a dark disorder, a moving chaos, the seed and death of all things, which opposes the mind's luminous and adult stability.[3]

What we must understand from this upheaval of history, is that its effects were massive. They were not merely technological and political but psychospiritual. For the last 500 years, in other words, we have been laboring under a peculiar kind of panic that I call the "chaos complex." This complex is pernicious—and we will do everything we can, even to the point of destroying ourselves, to repel it. Moreover, the chaos complex is a result of transgenerational trauma that you will not find in standardized textbooks; and yet it is starkly evident in our day-to-day lives.

For example, the frantic drive to foster convenience seems very much a vestige of this panic. Such pursuit has led to everything from fast foods to assembly line medicine, from patch-up mental health care to virtual friendships, and from violent videos to computerized war (or

---

[2] The 16th century definition of the color black is from Howard Zinn's *A People's History of the United States*, p. 31 (New York: Harper Perennial, 2015).

[3] "let us [consider]...madness..." Quoted in Foucault's *Madness and Civilization*, p. 13.

"riskless risk" as it was put by sociologist John Hannigan in a slightly different context. See his *Fantasy City: Pleasure and Profit in the Postmodern Metropolis*). We are surveilled and manipulated, boxed and branded—and many of us just saunter along. While the era of the singularity—where humans are rendered irrelevant—may still be a ways off, our humanity, the thing that brings us alive and makes us throb, may be at the precipice. The frank reality is that addiction to machines is exploding—and it is not too early to ask if the capacity for human touch, for imagination, for curiosity and for depth of relationships is dwindling (see again Turkle's piece on the decline of empathy).[4] The danger here, at least presently, is not the eradication of something urgently human, but the *atrophy* of deeply personal forms of expression as they are rapidly replaced by externalized mechanics. When body parts atrophy, they decay. And if they decay long enough, they not only shrink and disappear, they become erased from our collective memories, unavailable essentially to the functioning organism.

This then may be our main problem at present; that young people will no longer even recognize what they are missing; that the shift from requisite education in the arts and humanities, from "street" canniness to almost total technically-based knowledge will hardly be recognized; that the shift from face-to-face cultivation of relationships and creative play to virtual and predesigned contacts will become commonplace. In short, people won't know what they've never experienced—nor seen!

This, notably, is the world we're entering and it must be embarked upon with sobriety. We must not be naïve about it, because the governmental and industrial powers that be are largely blind to it—and for the sake of profits, they have every motive to be.

A Note on Metamodernism and the Irony of Contemporary Art

At the same time as so many of us are "buying into" the transhumanist revolution, there is a growing sensibility, particularly pronounced in film and rarified examples of protest, that vehemently questions the emerging trends. This movement may be called "metamodernist" because it transcends both modernist beliefs in technological salvation, as well as postmodernist stresses on total deconstruction of identity

---

[4] On the decline of empathy, see Sherry Turkle's "The Empathy Gap: Digital Culture Needs What Talk Therapy Offers."

which shows up in the nihilism implied in the transhumanist vision of the singularity. In essence, metamodernism is a self-conscious critique of both the naïve faith in technocracy, as well as the hopeless vision of nihilism.[5] It is akin to "metaconsciousness," the capacity to reflect on reflection, but on a cultural and metaphorical level. Metamodernism, for example, is illustrated by films such as *The Matrix, Her, Melancholia*, and *Birdman*. In these films the central characters all grow weary of the commodification and mechanization of life, and find ways to extricate themselves from or at least fight against the prevailing ethos. Documentaries such as the BBC's *Century of the Self* and *The Power of Nightmares*, as well as U.S. films, such as *The Corporation* are also illustrative of how the structures of power influence, and by implication, prompt us to reconsider our day-to-day lives.

Recently, in a haunting exhibit of metamodernist art at the de Young Museum in San Francisco, I came across a particularly striking sculpture. It was fashioned after a church entirely comprised of bullets. Now this work could be looked at in many ways, but what particularly impacted me was the ironic meld of cold technology (bullets) with nurturing shelter (the church). How many other ways, I thought, was our culture melding such apparent opposites? How many other ways does the remorselessness of technology encroach on our most intimate spaces? The work not only alerts us to the potential for a mechanized and weaponized sanctuary, but for a digitalized schoolroom, a cyber-hacked stateroom, or a text-messaged romance.

While these symbolic and occasionally literal protests are encouraging, they generally provide little guidance about how we might change course. This is a daunting problem, to be sure, but it is a problem that, despite its limitations, metamodernism can still address; for the more that we unveil about how we *presently* live, the more we can discover how we *desire* to live.

---

[5] The concept of "metamodernism" is drawn from M. Lemberger and T. Lemberger-Truelove's "Bases for a More Socially Just Humanistic Praxis." *Journal of Humanistic Psychology, 56,* 2016, pp. 571-580 and Luke Turner's "Metamodernism: A Brief Introduction." *Notes on Metamodernism.* January 12, 2015. Retrieved 2/10/17 from: http://www_metamodernism.com/2015/01/12/metamodernism-a-brief-introduction/

Chapter 3

The Problem with Normal Brains:
Neuroscience and Its Follies

In 1797, Francisco Goya painted a remarkable portrait. This was no ordinary portrait; but one with startling power that reverberates to this day. Simply put, the portrait depicts an artist slumped over his desk surrounded by beasts. The caption beneath the artist reads: "The Sleep of Reason Produces Monsters."

This ironic caption has one of the great double meanings in art. The first meaning appears to convey that when reason sleeps it can enable a bewildering world of beasts. The second meaning, on the other hand, seems to betray the contrary—that reason itself can be a form of sleep, and that by itself, or through its own machinations, can produce a world of monsters. Indeed, in a lucid postscript Goya writes that "Imagination abandoned by reason produces impossible monsters, united with her, she is the mother of the arts and the source of their wonders."[1]

For all their benefits, and there are many, the professions of psychiatry and psychology have largely overlooked Goya's warning. Instead, they have meticulously followed the machine model of psychological health. With precious exceptions, this model stresses regulation, linear thinking and adjustment to social norms, while almost entirely neglecting the challenges to these dimensions. Among these challenges are many whom history has shown to be vital and creative trailblazers; or if not trailblazers then ethically attuned, inventive people who "think outside the box," as the expression goes.

Enter neuroscience, the purported bedrock of the social sciences, which now buttresses just about every machine model of functioning. Consider the following from Dan Siegel, a prominent, well-meaning neuroscientist, on the "healthy" brain:

---

[1] Quote from "Goya, The Sleep of Reason Produces Monsters" by Sarah Schaefer, *Khanacademy*. Retrieved 12/26/16 from https://www.khanacademy.org/humanities/becoming-modern/romanticism/romanticism-in-spain/a/goya-the-sleep-of-reason-produces-monsters

> Through this synthetic analysis emerges the perspective that
> mental well-being is created within the process of integration,
> the linkage of differentiated components of a system into a
> functional whole. In this view ... we see that when a system's
> components become functionally linked—when they are
> integrated—they can be defined as having a FACES flow:
> flexible, adaptive, coherent, energized, and stable....In the flow,
> the experience is filled with COHERENCE: connected, open,
> harmonious, engaged, receptive, emergent, noetic,
> compassionate, and empathic.[2]

The problem with this now quite prevalent view is not that it is
inaccurate—indeed, just the contrary at given points. The issue
however is that it is *idealized,* and in a quite specific way. Stated bluntly,
Siegel's analysis reads more like a computer printout of well-being,
rather than a nuanced, intimate portrait of a life well lived. For example,
neural *experiences* are termed "systems" and "functionally linked
components." Optimal functioning is characterized as "coherent,
connected, open, harmonious, etc." But living *people*—even at their
peak—don't tend to "operate" so smoothly. Regardless of their neural
patterns on an MRI, even the hardiest among us are often frustrated,
despairing and helpless creatures. We/they are jumbles of
contradictions, tangles of ambivalence, and hair triggers of reactivity—
how can we help feeling these things at some level, knowing we're going
to die, not having a clue about our origins nor a hint of our destinations?
These are problems that will probably never show up on an MRI study,
or a precise neural configuration. But they are nevertheless intimately
experienced both in our day-to-day lives and in our therapy offices.

Moving too quickly to reduce complex experiences to neural
mechanics in psychotherapy is indeed a growing problem. Another
well-meaning mental health professional, the psychiatrist Frank
Anderson, lucidly articulates the trend. In an op-ed piece in the popular
Psychotherapy Networker, Anderson elaborates on the value of a
neurological analysis of post-traumatic stress:

> When clients experience sympathetic hyperarousal [during
> post-traumatic stress], the parts of their brain that can calm

---

[2] "Through this synthetic analysis..." is quoted from Dan Siegal's *The Mindful Brain:
Reflection and Attunement in the Cultivation of Well Being*, p. 288 (New York: Norton,
2007).

things down are shut down or offline. This is where therapists need to help them bring those parts of their brain back online. Monitoring your reactions while staying present and nonreactive allows you to be the "rational brain" in the room and helps your client shift out of danger into mindful curiosity.[3]

Again, while there is much accuracy in Anderson's analysis, two questions arise: 1) is the neurological, and even computerized, language Anderson uses necessary; and 2) does such a language have a mechanizing effect on how Anderson engages his clients, and thus potentially restrict the many layers of their intimately experienced worlds? Anderson uses terms like "staying present" and "mindful curiosity," but in my experience as a clinician these dimensions do not inexorably, or even necessarily ideally, lead to a "rational brain" where "hypersympathetic arousal" goes "offline." Indeed, the invitation of concerted presence can sometimes support clients to explore their "arousal" more fully, and to see the emancipatory value of *not* necessarily thinking so rationally. While I do not contest the value of helping *some* clients in certain contexts to learn emotional containment, the structure of Anderson's language implies that what is achieved medically, for example to halt diseased, pathogenic "brain parts," is equivalent to what must be done psychotherapeutically. This is a trivialization and in some cases outright subversion of optimal therapeutic change.[4]

Moreover, the problem of *experiential* health is also not readily identifiable on neurological assessments of the so-called normal or even optimal brain. By contrast, that which is found on such assessments are patterns of activity that may or may not tell us how people *perceive* these patterns—what anger or arousal or pleasure *mean* to people through the course of their lives. For example, an assessor may be able to gauge whether someone is active or passive,

---

[3] "When clients experience sympathetic hyperarousal..." is quoted from Frank Anderson's "Responding to extreme trauma symptoms: How neuroscience can help." *Psychotherapy Networker,* November/December, 2016, p. 15.

[4] Regarding the passage starting "This is a trivialization..." see David Elkins' superb summary of the latest psychotherapy outcome research in *The Human Elements of Therapy: A Non-Medical Model of Emotional Healing* (Washington, DC: American Psychological Association Press, 2016). This research points to personal and relational factors, such as the therapeutic alliance, empathy, collaboration, believability and hope as being far more significant than technical factors in the promotion of therapeutic effectiveness.

joyful or sad, aggressive or tranquil and the like. They may detect many neurological signals, but what they can't detect, without personally encountering a client, are the wealth of ways that given client frames those signals. How do they *experience* their anger—as a way of standing up to the world; as an impetus to freeing themselves from a degrading situation; or as a health-threatening compulsion, a lingering bitterness? Correspondingly, how does the client experience so-called passivity— as a contemplative pause; as a rejuvenating break; or as a victimization and onerous dependency? Without talking to clients and attempting to fully understand, what the assessor ends up with are oversimplifications and surfaces; not the multidimensional, paradoxical and ambivalent creatures we often are and need to be if we are to intensively live.[5]

Consider for example the experience of the sense of awe. Awe is formally defined as a commingling "of dread, veneration, and wonder;" it is a "cohabitation" of profound humility and sense of smallness juxtaposed to equally profound fascination and curiosity with life. Awe conveys humanity's sense of apartness from and participation in the grandeur of creation.[6] And yet, so far as I can tell, there is not one neural configuration that can register such elusive and intricate sensibilities. Here, for example, is St. Theresa's encounter with mystical awe:

> Beside me, on the left, appeared an angel in bodily form.... He was not tall but short, and very beautiful; and his face was so aflame that he appeared to be one of the highest rank of angels, who seem to be all on fire.... In his hands I saw a great golden spear, and at the iron tip there appeared to be a point of fire. This he plunged into my heart several times so that it penetrated to my entrails. When he pulled it out I felt that he

---

[5] Granted, there is an emerging field within neuroscience termed "neurophenomenology" which attempts precisely to combine intimate, in depth descriptions of human experience with precise neurological configurations. See for example the overview by B. Robbins and S. Gordon entitled "Humanistic neuropsychology: The implications of neurophenomenology for psychology" in *The handbook of humanistic psychology* (195-211) (Sage: 2015). While I applaud this development within the neuroscience field, I think we still must concede that it is the in depth, intimate descriptions—particularly from literature and the arts—that come closest to valid depictions of human experience, and that the physiological calculus, brilliant as it may be, is at best a placeholder for, and supplementation to, the former.

[6] Awe as defined by *Webster's New Collegiate Dictionary*. (Springfield, MA: Miriam-Webster, 1988) as well as K. Schneider in *Awakening to awe: Splendor, mystery, and the fluid center of life.* (Lanham, MD: Jason Aronson, 2009).

took them with it, and left me utterly consumed by the great
love of God. The pain was so severe that it made me utter
several moans. The sweetness caused by this intense pain is so
extreme that one cannot possibly wish it to cease, nor is one's
soul content with anything but God. This is not a physical but a
spiritual pain, though the body has some share in it—even a
considerable share.[7]

While this quote may seem extreme, it is, again, hardly unfamiliar to
anyone who has made a passionate commitment to something or
someone, and it is hardly traceable by neuroscientific mapping!
Consider, for further examples, the bitter-sweetness between lovers,
the birth of a baby, the creation of a project (such as this one), or even
the witnessing of a merciful death, as my wife and I experienced
recently with our beloved dog, Barty. These are all exceedingly
multifold moments, rife with immeasurable awe.

Another example of the incapacity of neuroscience to elucidate
sublime human experience is the virtually endless line of culturally
acknowledged inventors, creators and geniuses who display
paradoxical qualities. This state of affairs was graphically depicted in
an evocative book called *Touched with Fire*, by Kay Jamison. In this
groundbreaking study, some 200 of Western society's "Who's Who"—
from Lord Byron to Hans Christian Anderson, and from Michelangelo to
William James—were evaluated at the level of contemporary
psychodiagnostic functioning; and what Jamison found was that
virtually all 200 of the aforementioned qualified for bonafide
psychiatric conditions.[8]

Dean Keith Simonton and Ruth Richards, two other prominent
investigators of "greatness" found virtually the same themes.[9] What are
we to make then of these ostensibly conflicting findings? How do we
reconcile Siegel's "mindful brain" with its smoothly integrated system
of differential parts, with the typically "manic-depressive," agonizing
and ecstatic, profiles of social titans? How do we reconcile the findings
of neuroscience with the flawed, vital, inspiring and stunted people

---

[7] Quote beginning "Beside me, on the left..." is from E.A. Peers (Trans.), *The life of Teresa of Jesus: The Autobiography of Teresa of Avila* (New York: Doubleday, 1991, p.164).

[8] See Kay Jamison's *Touched with Fire: Manic-depressive Illness and the Artistic Temperament* (New York: Free Press, 1993).

[9] See Dean K. Simonton's *Greatness: Who Makes History and Why* (New York: Guilford, 1994).

many of us know? My conclusion is that we can't, and the sooner we get over our misplaced enthusiasm for those medically delimiting categories of normalcy, the better. The sooner we define neuroscientific data as *supplementary to and in some cases bolstering of* a larger psychology of mind, the better.[10]

On the other side of the ledger, neuroscience has little to tell us about the cause and nature of so-called psychopathologies; for just as neuroscience has defined as pathological that which many would view as normal or even resilient as noted above, equally, neuroscience has delineated normal ("healthy") as that which many would see as corrupt. Indeed there are very few states that neuroscience can confirm as mentally disordered, because again the issue of disorder resides more in the realm of experiential and cultural judgment rather than physiological damage.[11]

Take for example the following statements by people that neuroscientists would likely consider as possessing "normal brains":

- Alfred Rosenberg, an early spokesperson for Nazism, characterized Russian peasants as "half-idiotic, morose looking bastard variations of indefinable human types..."[12]
- Adolf Eichman, lieutenant colonel of the Third Reich, stated that "If of the 10.3 million Jews ... we had killed 10.3 million, I would be satisfied, and would say, 'Good, we have destroyed an enemy.... We would have fulfilled our duty to our blood and our people...'"[13]
- Christopher Columbus on the natives of the Bahaman Islands stated: "With fifty men we could subjugate them all and make

---

[10] See R. Richards' "Relationships Between Creativity and Psychopathology: An Evaluation and Interpretation of the Evidence" *Genetic Psychology Monographs, 103,* 1981, 261-304.

[11] The issue of "mental health problems" is increasingly seen as environmentally induced rather than the result of innate physiological dispositions. See J. Read and R.P. Bentall's "Negative Childhood Experiences and Mental Health: Theoretical, Clinical, and Primary Prevention," *British Journal of Psychiatry, 200,* 2012, 89-91.

[12] Alfred Rosenberg quote from R. Evans' *The Third Reich In Power* (New York: Penguin, 2006, p. 166).

[13] Adolf Eichmann quote from Bettina Stangneth (Translated from the German by Ruth Martin-Eichmann) *Before Jerusalem: The Unexamined Life OfA Mass Murderer* (New York: Alfred A. Knopf, 2014).

them do whatever we want."[14]

- Congresswoman and U.S. presidential candidate Michele Bachmann described homosexuality as "a very sad life. It's part of Satan, I think, to say that this [lifestyle] is gay."[15]
- President Vladimir Putin of Russia declared that the dismantling of the USSR "was the greatest geopolitical catastrophe of the 20th century."[16]
- Presidents George W. Bush and Lyndon B. Johnson preemptively attacked sovereign countries and compromised millions of lives on the basis of false and misleading evidence.[17]

Finally, consider R.D. Laing's 1967 observation that "normal men have killed perhaps 100 million of their fellow normal men in the past 50 years."[18] Neuroscience has no answer for that problem. Nor for how legions of normal brains (including some neuroscientists!) managed to endorse Hitler, or Stalin, or Pol Pot, or Mao, or Tojo, or the Christian Crusades, or the Inquisition, or Napoleon, or the British subjugation of India, or the U.S. invasions of Viet Nam and Iraq, and the list goes on and on. Today we have a "new normal" as the British filmmaker Adam Curtis put it in his BBC documentary "HyperNormalisation." It is the normalization of government leaders who equate entire ethnic groups with criminality, mock the disabled, and divide the world into "winners" and "losers." It is also the normalization of the millions who celebrate, or at best overlook these bewilderments.

The point is that in their present state, neither neuroscience nor organized psychology and psychiatry can get close to a satisfying definition of normality, or abnormality. The instruments with which they gauge such conditions are simply too crude—and as long as they rely on a machine model for their assessments, they are likely to remain

---

[14] Columbus quote from Howard Zinn's *A People's History of the United States* (New York: Harper Perennial, 2015, p.1).

[15] Bachman quote from G. Goldberg's "Bachman's Unrivaled Extremism." *The Daily Beast,* June 14, 2011. Retrieved 3/10/17 from http://www.thedailybeast.com/articles/2011/06/14/michele-bachmanns-unrivaled-extremism-gay-rights-to-religion.html

[16] Putin quote in R. Service's *A History of Modern Russia: From Tsarism to the 21st Century* (Cambridge, MA: Harvard University Press, 2009, p. 548).

[17] Bush and Johnson's fabricated wars from Kirk Schneider's *The Polarized Mind: Why It's Killing Us and What We Can Do About It.*

[18] Laing, R. D. (1967). *The Politics of Experience.* New York: Ballantine.

crude. The machine model takes the messy, vibrant world of bold and suffering lives and turns them into diagnostic and statistical clumps. It turns them into formulae that discount the paradoxes of living—such as the hostility that can be masked by glee or the budding resolve that can be obscured by despair.

The upshot is that the machine model can help people at the restrictive level of stabilization, but not at the level of the anxieties and yearnings that underlie the stabilization. What is the long-term outlook for such a direction? Far from the utopia of transhumanistic forecasts, I fear it will be the dystopia of unintended, and disturbingly intended, consequences. For even if such torments as criminality, megalomania, despair and terror can be technologically eradicated, new torments are likely to arise. Among these could be the agony of boredom, or of docility, or of indifference—for if you remove the aggressions, might you not also eradicate the passions and the boldness to risk? If you eliminate the sorrows and terrors, might you not also cede the sensitivities and creative possibilities for discovery?

These are real prospects, not simply the musings of a poetic sentimentality, and they go right to the problem of present trends as outlined in Chapter 2.

Even if neuroscience could titrate, that is tailor, aggression, fear and the like to manageable levels, who or what will decide what is manageable? And what does it mean to titrate brain functioning through drugs or genetic manipulation? Would such palliatives bypass the cultivation of natural capacities that form the basis for lasting or holistic change? For *dignified* change? For example, if person X received a drug to become more civil and well-integrated, would that individual grow to resent the fact that it was the drug and not his own energies and efforts that "made" him better? Would he become wooden and superficial because his experience transformed mechanically, and not mindfully, through hard-won steps? We see some of these problems with people who take medications today—their frenzies or sorrows are stemmed, but so are their joys and exuberances.

Or, on the other hand, what if neuroscience could create super-geniuses? Would they be able to develop the sensitivities and multi-dimensionalities of savants of the past? Einstein became a humanitarian in addition to being a brilliant physicist; but Einstein cultivated that former dimension through hard-won encounters from being a Jew in Nazi Germany, from the witnessing of wartime atrocities and countless other degradations. He did not develop those qualities through well planned reconfigurations of his brain or genetic reprogramming.

The lesson then is to tread very carefully when it comes to the neuro-medical cultivation of morality. The illumination of such a quality will not be optimized through a neuro-medical consensus. By contrast, it must be drawn from everyday, well-informed *people,* neuro-medical and otherwise; people who look over history and their own lives and forge a consensus about what humanity can, and should, be. In this light, I next sketch out a summary of humanistic/awe-based alternatives to the present trends. This is a preliminary guidepost to be sure, but it is a basis on which to build, and on which to usher in a new humanistic/awe-based era.

Chapter 4

A New Humanism in the Age of High Tech

Following the prophetic literary philosopher Thomas Mann, I propose "a new humanism" as a guide that may be helpful in our search for "what humanity can, and should, be." Humanism has a long and at times checkered history. However, I propose that it is now ready for a renaissance. I define this new humanism as the search for "what it means to be fully, experientially human, and how that understanding illuminates the vital and fulfilled life."[1]

Before looking at its implications for transhumanism, let us take some time to unpack this densely layered definition. First of all, by "new humanism" I mean a departure from the humanism that strictly emphasized individual gratification through rational principles of living. While I don't reject the delimited value of these principles, as noted above, I feel that they ironically have contributed to some of the very problems we find ourselves mired in by transhumanism. That is, transhumanism has extended certain outmoded humanistic values, such as isolated individualism and calculative, linear thinking to nightmarish proportions. The new humanism by contrast emphasizes a *search* for what it means to be human, signifying an openness to humanity's ever-evolving nature, and not some rigidified essence. That said, the new humanism also seeks that which is "fully, experientially human," meaning embracing our condition head on, without consolation, to the degree that it can be achieved; from our moldering fragility to our volcanic boldness; and from our estrangement with, to our participation in, the vast forces of existence. In an essay called *This I Believe*, just prior to the Second World War, Mann (1939) put it this way:

---

[1] Quote on the definition of humanistic psychology is from Kirk Schneider, F. Pierson, & J.F.T. Bugental (Eds.) *The Handbook of Humanistic Psychology: Theory, Practice, Research* (2nd ed.), (Thousand Oaks, CA: Sage, 2015, p. xvii).

I believe in the coming of a new ... humanism, distinct in complexion and fundamental temper from its predecessors. It will not flatter [humankind], looking at [him/her] through rose-colored glasses, for it will have had experiences of which the others knew not. It will have stout-hearted knowledge of [humanity's] dark, demonic, radically 'natural' side, united with reverence for [its] super-biological spiritual worth. The new humanism will be universal, and it will have the artist's attitude; that is, it will recognize that the immense value and beauty of the human being[s] lies precisely in the fact that [they] belong to the two kingdoms of nature and spirit. It will realize that no romantic conflict or tragic dualism is inherent in the fact, but rather a fruitful and engaging combination of determinism and free choice. Upon that it will base a love for humanity in which its pessimism and optimism will cancel each other.[2]

While the contents of this essay were written almost 80 years ago, their tenor could not be more relevant, or urgent. To be sure, we do operate on a level of mechanical physics, mathematical laws and neurobiological principles; but we also operate in some nonspecific, intuitive realm—a place of contradictory impulses and far-flung fantasies that form the crux of our awareness. This "crux" is best described by artists, poets and adventurers who help us come alive—people who draw upon whole body experience, as well as maximal absorption in whatever it is they endeavor.

How then does the new humanism respond to transhumanistic trends? What concrete steps are necessary to stem the technocratic tide? First, in my view, we need to make some tough choices about how we're willing to live. We need to realize that though we may enjoy devices that make the world more efficient—and that even may make us healthier and safer, they have their price, and we need to weigh that price against what is delivered. For example, one may crave the stimulation of a virtual reality video, say an adventure story in which the viewer is the hero, but at the same time one may recognize equally that an actual adventure, say on some weekend trip or in a romantic tangle, is a vital and necessary counterpart for a fuller and more

---

[2] The quote "I believe in the coming of a new..." is from Thomas Mann's *I Believe: The Personal Philosophies of Certain Men and Women of Our Time*, edited by C. Fadiman (New York: Simon & Schuster, 1939, p.193).

dignified life. Or as parents, we might take comfort in meticulously arranging a child's day, but we also might realize the exhilaration that child can experience by mapping out his or her own day, venturing into a pick-up game of soccer, or playing in sensuous mud. We might take our child out to the ocean or on a hike or encourage him or her to create games with friends. Of course, we can recognize the place for discipline and safety, but we also need to see that hyper-insulation can cripple a child—physically, emotionally and spiritually. Mounting studies, for example, show that immersion in nature is critical to child development, and that kids who are deprived of natural environments tend to become comparatively more stressed, distractible and aggressive.[3]

We might also choose to accept the challenge of raising a vulnerable, flawed child in place of a genetically engineered "designer child" who, on the surface at least, bears no defects. Now of course the issue becomes intensely complicated the further we move up the ladder of invulnerability. For example, researchers like Kurzweil may ask, if we have the means of replacing brain parts with computer chips, with accessing knowledge at speeds of unprecedented range and substance, and of creating body parts of virtually immortal resilience, why in heaven's name would we not use them!? Well, I'm not sure that we could, or even by most ethical rights, should, refuse to use them. The question is not binary—use them or not—it is deliberative: what are the contexts in which they should be used or not?

But more about alternatives to the transhumanist vision later. Presently, we're focused on the question of what it means to be fully, experientially human and how that sheds light on the vital or fulfilled life.

The Power of Paradox

It seems to me there is one overarching property that distinguishes human from nonhuman existence. And although hinted at earlier, this property may surprise many readers. It is not consciousness, because artificial intelligence is already showing that mechanical entities can achieve a kind of signal detection that simulates awareness—consider robots that register temperature changes in the environment. It is not

---

[3] For more on the effect of high tech on children's emotions see A. Novotney's "Smartphone: Not-So-Smart Parenting." *Monitor on Psychology*, February 2016, pp. 52-55.

reflexive consciousness, which is the ability of consciousness to have some level of awareness of itself, because scientists are already working on machines that can readjust their calculations based on incoming data; and it is not even the capacity to experience emotions because there are neural chips in development that will someday be able to replicate the biochemical processes that comprise say sadness or elation; which in crude form is possible today with psychotropic drugs. By contrast, the biggest if not insurmountable hurdle for artificial intelligence is a much more complicated problem—it is the experience of life's paradoxes. As with the testimony of St. Theresa referred to earlier, it is the experience not of a single image, thought or emotion, but of the sublimely interwoven image, thought and emotion; each of which can both dovetail and clash with one another.

Such paradoxes include the sliver of fear in a loving relationship, or the hint of sorrow in a moment of glee, or the taste of envy in the most admiring friendships; and it is many more, delicately subtle combinations that lend life its zest, it's pathos and it's intensity.

Machines simply cannot produce these virtually infinite intermixtures, and they therefore pale in that sense, before the intricacy of persons.

The result of these paradoxical intermixtures is that the new humanism is also an "awe-based" humanism. This is a humanness of *both* our worm-likeness and god-likeness—our humility *and* wonder, or sense of adventure toward living. Machine living cuts all that out; and it is predicated on cutting all that out.

Without the paradoxes of humanness, we would not be able to tap into life, because life itself is rife with paradoxes, such as creation and destruction, small forces and large forces, and the unchartable evolution of elements. Consider further, for example, each of the so-called negative emotions and how they echo these awesome ranges of awareness.

Sadness, for example, comprises sorrow and despondency, the profound sense of bereavement and loss. But post-traumatic growth studies also indicate that sadness alerts us to the fleeting nature of life, the preciousness of the moment, and the need for empathy for others' woes. Conversely, it serves as a point of comparison with, and therefore can help to intensify contrasting feelings, such as unbarred joy, elation and delight. As Rilke put it, sadness can bring something new to our experience that deepens it, and that deepening enhances our capacity to appreciate life.[4]

Fear. While fear diminishes and confines us, it also highlights that which towers over us. Certainly fear can humiliate, but research suggests that it also can sober us about what can and cannot be achieved.[5] Fear, likewise, acts as a backdrop for courage. For without fear, courage would mean little and likely impact little in the course of our lives. Would we even seek to be courageous if we had no fear?

Would we seek new fields, and fresh thoughts, sensations, or innovations without encountering some degree of fear? These questions are rarely asked by enthusiasts of transhuman technologies.

Anger. This emotion arouses danger, explosiveness and domination. It is a fiery blast, and an expansion that threatens decimation of others.

But informed studies also show that anger is a way of standing up for oneself as in righteous indignation; it is an impetus to courage and rejuvenation of spirit.[6] Invigorating revolutions have upwelled from anger, and so have personal liberations. Without anger, tenderness may be thin, the poignancy of kindness unnoticed.

Envy. Coveting the qualities of another is the seedling of envy; obsessing over and fantasizing about possessing those qualities is the blossoming of envy. Envy arouses desperation to be something other than what one is; it is a maddening torment. But my experience as a therapist, as well as client, has shown me that envy is also an aspiration, a prospect, and a potentially life-changing breakthrough. We see the glimmers of our desires in those we envy and thereby have some capacity to nurture those desires. Envy contrasts with contentment, and, by way of contrast, lends contentment its restorative depth.

Guilt alerts us to words or deeds we regret. It is a "hammer" in the depths of conscience and it pummels all forms of complacency. Guilt dims our acceptability and dashes our esteem. At the same time, as studies of psychopathy have shown, guilt, and its social counterpart, shame, jars us to improve, apprises us of our potentiality to do better,

---

[4] See R.M. Rilke's *Letters to a Young Poet* (Norton, New York, 1993). See also studies of "depressive realism" such as L. Alloy and L. Abramson's "Depressive Realism: Four Theoretical Perspectives" in L. Alloy and L. Abramson (Eds.) *Cognitive processes in depression* (New York: Guilford, 1988, pp. 223-265).

[5] For more on fear and post-traumatic growth see R. Tedeschi and L. Calhoon's *Trauma and Transformation: Growing In The Aftermath of Suffering* (Thousand Oaks, CA: Sage,, 1995).

[6] For more on the liberating potential of anger see S. Diamond's *Anger, Madness, and the Daimonic* (Albany, NY: SUNY Press, 1996).

and moves us to heal others' wounds.[7] It's hard to inspire change if we fail to encounter guilt.

Literary Insights

The luminaries of literature and the arts also intimately knew of the paradoxes of emotion.[8] Great classics from *Oedipus Rex* to *Don Quixote* to *Divine Comedy* to *Faust* to *The Great Gatsby* to films like *Vertigo, Ikiru, Melancholia* and *The Great Beauty* are all about defying a machine model of living, either focused on the strivings or warnings of the protagonist.

In Sophocles' *Oedipus Rex* and *Oedipus at Colonus* we find the human being's encounter with fate. The fate in this case is Oedipus's horrific and unwitting destruction of his father, King Laius, in a roadside accident, which then leads through a series of mishaps to the wedding and subsequent marriage of Oedipus with his mother Jocasta. The upshot however is that when Oedipus, now King Oedipus, learns of the debacle, he is overcome with guilt and self-loathing, which in turn drives him to blind himself as if blocking himself entirely from the tragedy. But with time he finds he cannot succeed, just as none of us can succeed ultimately to deny that which we regret, and are challenged either to live with it or self-destruct. In classic literary fashion, Oedipus chooses to live with his tragedy, though blind and hobbled to a contented old age. Oedipus finds a way to cohabitate with, that is, accept the paradoxes of his (our) condition.

In Cervantes' *Don Quixote* we have an ostensibly maniacal dreamer who fights with windmills and courts an unattainable woman, Dulcinea. But this eccentric and devalued "fool" is also a passionate and vibrant fool; a person who stepped "out of the box" of routinized living, and found a wonder-filled world. Deluded as he may be in the conventional life, Don Quixote acquired insights and ambitions—his "heavenly cause"—that dwarfed the gentlemen of nobility!

With Dante Alighieri's *Divine Comedy*, we find Dante at midlife "lost in a dark wood." He is wracked with sin and self-doubt, spiraling into hell's tormenting rings. But the other side of the story is that Dante

---

[7] The power of guilt is explored in Rollo May's *The Cry for Myth* (New York: Norton, 1991).

[8] The paradoxes of emotion in art and literature are vividly elucidated by Rollo May in *The Cry for Myth* (New York: Norton, 1991) and Kirk Schneider's *Horror and the Holy: Wisdom Teachings of the Monster Tale* (Chicago: Open Court, 1993).

decides to face his hell, grapple with each torment, and along the way acquire an unflappable helper, Virgil, to support his journey. What *Divine Comedy* foretells is that by staying present to one's sense of lostness, one's divergence from the crowd, one may find openings there, even treasures, that enlarge one's world. Through Virgil's therapist-like accompaniment, Dante learns that he is more than his surfeit of sins, but rather a creature of the cosmos, as it were, a divine spark in an otherwise bewildering existence, that can find his way anew as reflected in the angel-like character of Beatrice.

Goethe's *Faust* tells us of another bewildered and self-tormented soul, a learned professor no less, who feels he has wasted his life. He finds that his books and scholastic knowledge equate with the dreary and dust-filled halls of his academic tower. His life is gray, tired and old; and yet he longs for color, vigor and youth. Faust is the classic middle-aged depressive who no longer knows why or wherefore he toils. Then he meets *Mephistopheles*, the wise and clever devil who offers him a second chance. However, to accept that chance, the chance to become youthful and sensual and dynamic again, he must give up his ability to return to his sedentary and in some ways serene existence. It's as if the devil is saying "you want youth, you want wild, you want abandon? You'll get everything you think you want but there's no turning back." So in his desperation to expand, to be great without limits, Faust sets out to commit to the devil's pact. But what makes the play *Faust* so great is that it shows in no faint fashion how problematic one-way living can be. It was lousy when Faust was a dried up old academe and as he soon sees, it can be horrific reclaiming wild, reckless youth—he makes an underage girl pregnant, kills her protective brother, and drives her to virtual madness—until the last chapters when he realizes his excessive ways.

The upshot of *Faust* is that to be fully human we need to coexist with our dueling natures; we need to see that cut off from our youthful passions, we can become moribund, but abandoning ourselves to our fantasies, be they sensual or mechanistic, we can become psychopaths. The key from this standpoint is to acknowledge a portion of both, our humility *and* our wonder, our worm-likeness *as well as* our god-likeness, which save us not from death, as Faust learned only too well, but from living death.

The Great Gatsby by F. Scott Fitzgerald presents a similar foray into the paradoxical soup. Born and bred as an itinerate street kid, Jay Gatsby finds a way—both nefarious and officious—to earn riches. But his wealth and industriousness come at a very high price—the loss of sensitivity, of patience, of reflection on life, and in short, of soul. The return of his old beau Daisy is a chance for him to rekindle some of those former stirrings, but the stirrings cannot be rekindled—at least to his satisfaction. He cannot recapture what has been lost, and, unlike his stock market dealings, what has been lost is beyond his ability to recapture. He thus dies in the end, a broken man, and yet one who could glimpse the fuller and deeper horizon that lies just ahead. *The Great Gatsby* showed that militaristic and materialistic acquisition can carry a person only so far; the life of indulgence, debauchery and surface celebration can bring only so much zeal—and then the hollowness kicks in, the inner deadness. In the end, *Gatsby* shows us that money without meaning—wonder, creativity—and sex without intimacy pale before the possibilities of genuine living; and finally, *Gatsby* shows us that practicality must meet vision, and that vision ultimately is something sanctified not commercialized.

Turning to film, *Vertigo*, directed by Alfred Hitchcock is a model of paradoxical insight. Without belaboring the details (which I have elaborated on elsewhere[9]), *Vertigo* sets a disabled police officer, played by Jimmy Stewart, against a dizzying array of characters who are both oppressive and liberating. The main character in this maze-like drama is a dazzling blonde played by Kim Novak, who lures Stewart into her enigmatic lair. The upshot of the film however is that Stewart must learn to steer a middle path, neither catering to his victimization nor swooning into rapture, and that the power to thrive lies in the between; vulnerable and yet bold.

Ikiru, directed by Akira Kurowsawa and based on the Tolstoy novel *The Death of Ivan Illich,* is a poignant tale of an orderly bureaucrat who learns most about living at the moment he learns he is dying. All of his adult life Mr. Watanabe, the film's protagonist, has led an oblivious life. He ate, he slept, he said goodbye to his family, and he reliably went about his work. But the day comes when Mr. Watanabe learns that he is dying, and that is a day that turns around everything. Like every person eventually, Mr. Watanabe awakens to his mortality, and this consciousness alters every moment that he breathes. But ironically this is also where Mr. Watanabe's life becomes energized—almost beatific in fact; for the specter of death intensifies virtually all that Mr. Watanabe sees, touches and thinks about. Toward the end of the film,

---

[9] For my earlier work on *Vertigo* see Kirk Schneider, "Hitchcock's Vertigo: An Existential View of Spirituality" in the *Journal of Humanistic Psychology, 33,* pp. 91-100, 1993.

we see Mr. Watanabe paying close attention to life, but particularly those things that bring poignancy and freshness—a meal with an animated young lady, his son's room with so many joyous mementos such as the baseball bat that his child used to cherish, the happy children at the neighborhood playground, and even the swooping movement of the playground swing that Mr. Watanabe wistfully, but playfully engages.

Lars von Trier's *Melancholia* takes us to new levels of paradoxical awareness. The film begins with a lovely couple gleefully approaching a mansion for a massive celebration of their wedding. The mansion turns out to belong to the bride's sister, played by Charlotte Gainsbourg and her husband, played by Kiefer Sutherland. The whole story begins to go awry however as we home in on all the parties assembled. The bride, played by Kirsten Dunst, is increasingly agitated by, and blatantly estranged from, the superficial lavishness of the entire scene. Her sister is rigid and formal, yet curdling inside, her husband is both presumptuous and arrogant in the style of the nouveau riche, and Dunst's betrothed seems lost and monotonous. The net effect of these blows is that the allegedly disturbed and agitated Dunst—the "madwoman" of the household—appears to see through to the largest truth. This truth that escapes the blathering and self-assured partygoers, as well as the contemporary culture from which they emerge, is that humanity is a speck in the vastitude of nature and our lives but a spark. So much of our time is squandered on petty bickering, identities and pretention. Yet, the maelstrom surrounds us, either in death or in cosmic fate. As the film evolves to its climax, it becomes increasingly evident that Dunst's fears of humanity's fragility (ludicrous material obsessions and arrogant scientistic presumptions) are all valid, that a catastrophe awaits, and that the best we can do is to live with presence, vitality and compassion.[10]

The Great Beauty is another film for our times, though it's set in an exclusive community in Rome, punctuated by a host of colorful misfits. The film focuses on an aging one-hit wonder named Jep, played by Toni Servillo. Jep, we are shown, is a wealthy magazine writer who now dwells among the aristocrats and partiers of Rome, but who once was a serious and best-selling author. Jep is ambivalent. On the one hand he

---

[10] For an elaboration on von Trier's *Melancholia* see Kirk Schneider's "From Despair and Fanaticism to Awe: A Post-Traumatic Growth Perspective on Cinematic Horror" in D. Sullivan and J. Greenberg (Eds.) *Death in Classic and Contemporary Film* (New York: Pallgrave-Macmillan, 2013, pp. 217-229).

revels in the high life of the city, thrills at his carefree existence, and delights in his bon mots with friends, but on the other, he is sickened; there is a dull and growing regret for all that he has passed up since his youth. This ache sheds powerful light on the falseness of his and his fellows' meanderings, the emptiness of their chatter, and the futility of their long forsaken dreams. The conscious stem of this dream for Jep began when he was a youth of 17 and met his first love for whom he never—to his chronic regret—pursued. But the borders of the dream were much larger than an unrequited romance; they were the rays of life itself, the trembling beauty of life itself, through which he also skirted for many indulgent years. His writing captured a glimpse of these rays, but he forsook it for the fame and flare that followed, and hence began his Faustian path. Toward the end of the film, we find Jep increasingly wistful about that first tender love, but more importantly about the fuller life that he rebuffed. Yet, he sees that fuller life in the most surprising people, such as a 104-year-old Catholic nun whose wonder in the midst of hypocrisies is infectious. He sees it on his walks through the city, on strolls through ennobling statuary, and in the reemergence of his literary mind. With the closing scenes, however, Jep cherishes life itself, his participation in life itself, beyond his shriveling façade.

Lest one conceive that the paradoxes of emotion, the awe-based life, is confined to the classic art of the West, think again. The classic art of the East and regions South are also charged with these sensibilities.

The Taoist tale of the Chinese farmer is a case in point: An old farmer's horse runs away one day and the townspeople gather round him and express what a misfortune this is for him. But the old farmer replies, "maybe." Then the horse returns one day and the same townsfolk gather round the old farmer to convey how delightful this day must be to him, but the old farmer says, "maybe." Then the farmer's son decides to take the horse on a ride and breaks his leg. Again, the townsfolk gather round the old farmer to exhort what a tragedy this is for him and his boy. But the old farmer turns to them and says, "maybe." Then a cavalry of men ride up to the boy to conscript him into the army. However, when they see that he has damaged his leg they turn back. The townspeople gather round the farmer again and relay what good news this must be for him and his boy ... and the farmer says, "maybe." As can be seen from the above, the old farmer is wary of pat answers.

He knows that life is variable and that it is rarely wise to presume. The more discerning, and perhaps ennobling way, is to appreciate the joys and difficulties of the moment and leave the future to the fates.

There are also numerous stories from Buddhist lore that echo these kinds of paradoxes, and we can find similar stories in the Native American, Hispanic and African traditions as well. Such stories emphasize the limits of our ability to control nature, but also, and paradoxically, the expanse of our capacity to coexist with and find ways to participate in nature. Such interdependence is the hallmark of wisdom traditions the world over.[11]

---

[11] For more on Buddhist, Native American, Hispanic and African folk traditions that embrace life's paradoxes see L. Hoffman, H. Cleare-Hoffman, and T. Jackson's "Humanistic Psychology And Multiculturalism: History, Current Status, And Advancements" in K. Schneider, F. Pierson, & J.F.T. Bugental (Eds.) *The Handbook of Humanistic Psychology: Theory, Practice, Research* (2nd ed.) (Thousand Oaks, CA: Sage, 2015, pp., 41-56) as well as L. Hoffman, M.Yang, F. Kaklauskas, and A. Chan's *Existential Psychology East-West* (Volume 1: Revised and Expanded Edition) (Colorado Springs, CO: University Professors Press, 2019).

Chapter 5

From the New Humanism to Awe:
It's Time for a Cross-Cultural Spirituality

What we need to realize is that the complement to transhumanism is awe. If we can set our sites on the humility and wonder or sense of adventure toward living—the astonishment toward living—we will make two major course corrections. First, we will combat the polarization, the desperate quest for *certainty* that has plagued humanity from the start. While such a quest has granted us temporary solace, it has also almost invariably led to misery, both individually and collectively.

Second, awe-based consciousness can offset the present polarization of rationalism, which has incrementally led to the transhumanist illusion of godhood. The transhumanist illusion of godhood, or what the ancient Hebrews trenchantly called "idol worship" and the ancient Greeks "hubris," is the menacing bane of the present age. It is also the horror potentially of the age to come. I much prefer Huston Smith's notion of a "post-secular humanism" as the watchword of our coming age. This humanism embraces *both* the riches of religiosity, such as the awe for existence, *along with* the scientific spirit of inquiry.

Transhumanism and Terror: A Conceivable Cross-Road

The more we court machines, the more machine-like we become. The more we emphasize calculation, technique and quantity, the more calculating, technical and quantitative we become. It did not take a scholar to see this problem at the start of the 18th century and it does not take a savant to see the problem now. While many people don't write poems about the problem, or feature it in classic literature, you can be sure they sense it, and shudder at its ferocity. Again, industrialization has fostered many advances in standards of living, convenience and abilities to survive. But it has also fueled enormous capacities to destroy and humiliate; and not only at the level of cultures, but also at the level of dignity, character and identity.

Today we see the seedlings of transhumanism in everything from weaponry to gun ownership, tech-addiction to job regimentation, and consumerism to the corporate control of nature. We're not breaking backs in our over-mechanized, over-hyped techno-universes; we're breaking souls. But we also see a backlash against these developments, and some of these are constructive and restorative; while others are hair-raising and cataclysmic.

We don't often associate terror with the high tech, high convenience lifestyle, but terror is *not only what can be created* by that lifestyle, for instance through automaton-like citizenry, conscience-bereft criminality, and potentially self-guided robotics; terror is *also what can be opposed* to that hollow and demoralized lifestyle. This form of terror for example can be seen in religious movements that destroy secular monuments such as the World Trade Center towers; or that ban commercial music. While I am *not* suggesting that the mechanizing of humanity is the main reason for such terrorism, what I am saying is that elements of such terrorism are a backlash against, and in their own perverse way, an attempt to thwart mechanized modernity.

When the religious theorist and future founder of the Muslim brotherhood Sayyid Qutb visited the United States in the early 1950s, he was appalled at what he saw: box-like houses on prefabricated lawns, isolated individuals, and billboard-studded communities. These "abominations" in his view were accompanied by meaningless adornments and trash-lined streets; the message seemed to be "Just go to work, feed and protect your family, and prize your material gains." It was not on the other hand to "care for the environment, acknowledge your fellow human beings, and revel in the spectacle of life, the universe, and God."[1] Think what one may of Qutb's rather pious and heavy-handed views—he did have a point. He was alarmed by what he saw as the growing bankruptcy of industrialized life, the resultant irreverence, arrogance and flatness of that life, and the wholesale rejection of religious tradition, such as his native Islam.

While I contend that terrorism—and the need to inflate oneself—is primarily a defense against perceived helplessness—which many in

---

[1] Paraphrase of Sayyid Qutb is from http://en.wikipedia.org/wiki/Sayyid_Qutb as well as his essay "The America I Have Seen" retrieved January 27, 2017 at: https://archive.org/stream/SayyidQutb/The%20America%20I%2 0have%20seen _djvu.txt

Qutb's native Egypt experienced through the harsh rule of their leaders and the colonial powers who controlled those leaders—it is also, arguably, an ill-fated lunge at the sacral. Hence "awe-depletion" may court many levels of anguish, including the perversion of awe.[2]

The Spirituality of Awe and Transhumanism: Another Conceivable Cross-Road

The question then is how do we acknowledge the march of technical development, the transhumanist revolution, along with the furthering of emotional development at the same time? Is it possible for technical enhancement to exist side-by-side with awe-based consciousness? My answer is not only "yes" but that the combination is imperative. It is imperative because it is unrealistic and oppressive to believe that technological development can be staunched; just as it is foolhardy to overlook the necessity of emotional and awe-based deepening. We have seen societies and individuals who cut off one side or the other, and they become devitalized or obsolete. Our Western society is now in the former category. As we become smarter about devices, we seem to become dimmer about how our devices affect lives.

The spirituality of awe crosscuts the modern, the premodern and the postmodern. The humility and wonder, and sense of adventure toward living is a cornerstone of every major moral, ethical, scientific and religious worldview in the contemporary world. And yet we fail, by and large, to see what is directly in front of our noses. If we begin with awe, we see that it is foundational to an ethically and morally grounded science; just as it is foundational to an ethically and morally grounded religion. We see further that, in their essence, religion and science complement one another for the following reasons: 1) they both appreciate the mystery of existence; 2) they both prioritize a humility before the vastness of existence; 3) they both prize the depth and intricacy of existence, as well as the gift of life; and finally 4) they both cherish the contemplation of and connection with nature. To vivify these aforementioned points, consider the following religious and scientific credos:

---

[2] For a fuller discussion of the consequences of awe-depletion and demoralization, see Kirk Schneider's *The Polarized Mind: Why It's Killing Us and What We Can Do About It.* See also Hubert Dreyfus' *What Computers Still Can't Do: A Critique of Artificial Reason* (Cambridge, MA: MIT Press, 1992).

- Embrace the stranger/ Don't be afraid to investigate the strange or unusual
- Love thy neighbor as thyself/Philosophy as the love of wisdom; wisdom as love for all life
- Walk humbly and mercifully with the Lord/ Recognize one's limits, protect human and nonhuman life, appreciate the astonishing beyond
- Practice tolerance/ Emphasize openness to diverse data
- Accept mystery and paradox/ Be open to not knowing and contradictory findings
- People who live in glass houses shouldn't throw stones/ Think critically about your own assumptions
- My house has many mansions/ There are many interpretations of data
- Be wary of false idols/ Be skeptical of simplistic answers

And let us not forget Einstein's dictum: "Religion without science is blind, but science without religion is lame."[3]

The cultivation of a sense of awe despite and in light of high tech must take root at many levels; otherwise it devolves. In the sections to follow, we will look at how the sense of awe and high tech can coexist in five major sectors of living—childrearing, education, the work setting, the religious and spiritual setting, and government. Although I have touched on these areas in earlier work, I have not tied them explicitly to the high tech/transhumanist pull that challenges them at every turn.

Childhood and High Tech: Starting Out With Awe

The sense of awe begins at birth—I think most of us can agree on that. From the moment one is "tossed" into the world, one senses both humbleness (shock) and wonder (fascination) toward all that surrounds one. It doesn't get much more human than that.

Quite rapidly, moreover, at least in industrialized societies, infants perceive bright lights, hospital décor and sophisticated instruments; and in some sense these too must seem awesome. No less awesome in

---

[3] Einstein quote from Walter Isaacson's *Einstein: His Life and Universe* (New York: Simon & Schuster, 2007, p. 390).

all societies are the faces that begin to come into view, the outlines of bodies, and typically loving expressions. All these converge to both soothe and jar the emerging being.

In mechanized societies then childhood and high tech begin together; they interweave and converge at the moment of awe. In non-mechanized societies, faces, bodies and expressions converge at the moment of awe. In all societies therefore, awe is the base, the foundation on which much in this world revolves. Awe is also the birthright of a life-philosophy or sadly, of a fleeting glimmer bathed in amazement, charged with intensity.

The question as to how and when a child cultivates their sense of awe rides largely on the way they are treated by the world, and in particular by his or her caretakers. The world can crush this core sensibility or it can, within degrees, help to foster and deepen it. The world can act as a guide and nurture the child toward application of his or her awe in the service of humanity/life; or it can steamroll him or her into frameworks of its own making, pounding him or her into roles and categories that form the basis of a frustrating and embittered existence devoid of depth, bereft of significance. Or, of course, the world can promote many gradations in between, with varying degrees of impact.

The child's disposition no doubt is also a notable contributor to how they are treated by the world. Yet there is very little we can do about that disposition, while there is much that we can do about the world. If we accept the power of awe-based inspiration, promise and service to the world, the question is how do we encourage the nurturance of these qualities by the world? We've already established that high tech, elements of the transhuman ideology, can be a part of an awe-nurturing world—again, they are inherent to such a world. The way they are used however is the all-encompassing issue, and the way they are used harkens back to children's caretakers.

Caretaker attachment style, we now know, is integral to child development. The degree to which this attachment style is close or distant, supportive or neglectful, empathic or degrading, has major effects on the stability, regulating capacity and self-esteem of children. To the extent an attachment style is over- or under- attentive to a child's needs, that child is likely to become over- or under-attentive to his or her own needs and those of others. [4] In sum, to the degree that

---

[4] For an elaboration on attachment styles, see M.D.S. Ainsworth, M.C. Blehar, E. Waters, & S. Wall (1978) *Patterns of Attachment: A Psychological Study of the Strange Situation.* (Hillsdale, NJ: Erlbaum).

caretakers' attachment style promotes security, to that extent a child is also likely to feel secure and empowered in the world about him or her; to the degree that caretakers' attachment style fosters insecurity, to a proportional extent, a child too is likely to feel insecure and victimized by life.

This is all well and good; we need secure attachment styles to raise secure kids. However, from an awe-based view there is much more to consider here than parental attachment style—there is the whole question of how a child feels in relationship to existence as a whole, not just toward the particular person or people who raise him or her. One can feel secure and empowered in the world and yet conform one's behavior to the rationalistic, mechanistic lifestyle of contemporary society. This is a lifestyle that knows and cares little about the marvels of earth, sky and cosmos. One may be securely attached to familiar groups but quite shakily disposed to foreign or unusual people, to careers or lifestyles that are off the beaten track, to inquiry and creative thinking, and to love in its deepest and most diversified forms. Now attachment theorists might counter that precisely because they are secure, securely attached individuals tend to be more capable than insecurely attached individuals of tolerating differences, opening to strange or unusual situations, and generating innovative ideas.

In my view, this contention has merit; but only to the extent that those so-called securely attached individuals have been exposed to a kind of security that exceeds the basic kindness, centeredness and supportiveness of those close at hand, and that extends to the larger world and ultimately to the universe, beyond those personalities. In other words, I would like to emphasize the centrality of that which is called "ontological security/insecurity"—or security/insecurity with existence as a whole—beyond what has traditionally been called secure or insecure interpersonal attachment. In my view, it is the *ontologically* attached child who has been supported to venture out in the world, to grapple with feeling lost, and to contend with unknowing—who has the greater chance to become an awe-inspired, inquiring and diversely engaged adult.

What we are talking about here is the parental premium placed on *presence*, whether it is through the astonishingly intricate relationship with children themselves, or with the stories, puzzles, games, outdoor ventures, and peer activities that children are supported to pursue. To the extent that children can cultivate presence, they can also develop spiritual sustenance; or a larger view of what can be done and experienced in the world.

I invite you now to consider a couple of personal examples. The first is my own experience of awe through a television show about a high-tech creature, and the second is an episode of awe I experienced playing a low-tech neighborhood game.

As I noted earlier, I had a very troubled childhood. My brother died at seven years old and my world and that of my parents went into a tailspin. I had many terrifying nights and unsettling days. But what I learned through the "life-saving" conversations, therapies and literal as well as figurative "holding" from my parents, was gradually how to become present to myself and the world around me, gradually how to become intrigued, even fascinated by feeling lost at times, by experiencing the unsettling, the mysterious. These realizations bring to mind two memories that have been forever emblazoned in my heart. One was a growing fascination with science fiction programs, which were very good in those days in the early 1960s. Amid my fear, which I'm sure I was also trying to work through, I became increasingly intrigued by the aliens, scientists, strange forces and wild possibilities depicted on such programs as *The Twilight Zone, One Step Beyond,* and *The Outer Limits.* One episode of *The Outer Limits* stood out for me. It was an early show starring Cliff Robertson as a radio station operator. As he manned the station, he began to notice unusual interference patterns on his audio equipment. As time went on it suddenly became clear that a being, probably from very far away had gotten caught in the signals from his station and was trying to break through. Toward the end of the episode, the being did finally break through and was as tall as the radio tower. The being was an electrified "monster" who began lumbering through the local village, terrifying hordes of people who witnessed it. In the center of town where the being was headed, a large crowd amassed and amid that crowd were members of the military poised with machine guns and tanks. As the being approached, the crowd became increasingly distraught and the army mobilized for action. But then a very peculiar thing happened. The being suddenly stopped, looked down at the crowd and spoke in distorted but audible words: "Put down your guns, go home, and contemplate the mysteries of the universe!"

That was all the being said and that was the end of the program. What struck me on that day and even more so looking back is how brilliantly awe-based that story was. Here you have a terrifying stranger, a creature that fills us with dread and entirely throws us out of our comfort zone, and yet shows us just the opposite of what we fear. It exhibits to us that what we initially perceive may not actually be what is there, and what is there is not the killer that we thought it was, but a being, a presence from an unknown origin that reminds us to respect the unknown. It reminds us to put down our defensive armor just for a moment, collect our breaths, and try as best we can to be present to the MORE that is out there—beyond our narrow identifications and "secure" attachments to things. Even with high tech, there is a world of mystery to be explored, contemplated and adamantly celebrated.

My second example of presence to the MORE is also from my childhood and concerns a game called "Cops and Robbers." In this game, one team of kids would play the "cops," and the other "robbers." The cops would divide into two groups—one which played "guards" and the other which played cops in hot pursuit. The guards stood by at the "jail," which was really someone's garage, and the pursuing cops would disperse all over the neighborhood (usually confined to one street) to look for the robbers. The robbers, correspondingly, were one team of kids who looked for and found all kinds of hiding places between and around houses. The goal of the game was for the cops to find and tag a robber who would then be immediately escorted to jail. The game would end when the cops brought all the robbers into jail, which was not an easy task, because the whole scenario took place at night, I mean pitch-black night. And this was the exciting thing about it for both sides—cops would spread out into the blackness of the neighborhood, dodging rocks and hurtling through branches to find their adversaries, while the adversaries, the robbers, would have 10 seconds at the start of the game to venture deep into the grassy, tree studded backyards and hide. I remember the thrill of running free through the neighborhood and finding my secret spot to hide; or cagily dashing into unexpected alleys or fields to find robbers mysteriously eluding our grasp. The whole thing was basically about feeling and sensing the *mystery* of dark skies and obscure places, of the chill and yet thrill of surprise that may be just around the corner, and of the joy of comradeship as we explored and tussled together.

These then were some of my awe-based experiences both interacting with and outside of the technological world. I am sure that many children from a range of cultures share similar experiences in different forms, in very different settings. The issue here however is the cultivation of a certain attitude toward living. This attitude is very difficult to acquire without support for one's freedom, imagination and some manageable degree of anxiety. At the same time, it is very difficult to acquire without support and a sense that one can manage or be present to undiscovered thoughts, feelings and sensations. The "base" provided by parents and society is critical, not only at the level of interpersonal trust but at the level of trust in one's being, one's acceptability within the groundlessness of that which is foreign to one, or out of one's comfort zone. This sensibility takes a sustained period to take root, and that is why, optimally, it is supported from a very young age, within comparatively stable environments.

Of course, the world is full of unstable environments and untrustworthy people, and that is precisely why, as noted earlier, this awe-based project must address many levels of social functioning well beyond childhood and throughout formal schooling and careers. If the complete cycle is not pursued, we may have awe-informed children but they will be beaten down by awe-depleted systems, or we'll have awe-inspired adults debased by awe-deprived jobs, governments or religious strictures. The best way is if it can all work as a self-reinforcing, interlinking mosaic in which mechanization certainly has its place, but does not overshadow awe.

Returning to childhood then, what we are increasingly seeing in mechanized and even not so mechanized societies, is that kids are becoming obsessed with their devices. Whether it is texting, the internet, or Facebook, it seems that presence is going the way of fireside chats. Or maybe what kids are engaging in is a different kind of presence, a darting and strategic one, with nary a moment to pause. The rub however is that this addictive attention, this enchantment with techniques, is a harbinger of transhumanism. The more that children become schooled in mechanical play and machine-mediated awareness, the more they will be primed to adopt machine-like relationships, lifestyles and aspirations. We don't have to look far to see these developments today—take any random moment in large cities and you will see major portions of the population looking down at their cell phones. You will see them continually checking their cell phones. You will see them "surfing" on them, texting brief and too often inane messages on them, and you will see them have great difficulty sustaining attention apart from those "accompanists." More troubling you will see fully grown adults shifting back and forth with dinner companions, or family members, or even therapists to engage with their cell phones, and to make sure that they have not overlooked anything on their phones.

The question of where all this is leading is not that difficult to see. In addition to narrowing attention spans in families, schools and job sites, the obsessive preoccupation with handheld devices is bringing the entire question of critical thinking and scholarship to the fore. How will youth become "thinkers" if they are continually scattered or distracted, or if they lack the patience to really work a subject in depth? How will people see the bigger picture of their lives, those who are influencing their lives, and those who have come before them who may give them insight into their lives, if there is little or no ability to separate from, and look as if from above, that within which they are embedded? This is the core challenge that we face today and moving into the future. How are we to help children develop meta-awareness, or awareness of the more of who they are and have the potential to become?

This brings us to the problem not so much with technology per se, but with how technology is approached both emotionally and philosophically. In other words, we need to help kids to develop capacities for pausing, and for reflecting *in between* their preoccupation with devices. These capacities will help kids to be able to step back and consider what it is they're doing and who or what they're relating to. Again, these dimensions can lead to a fascination—even awe—toward machines but equally to a healthy skepticism about how machines may be ruling peoples' lives. The thrust of the issue then is to support kids to slow down, to think about their engagements with the world, their relationships with others, and their part in society as a whole, to the degree that they are ready. These suggestions are not about pushing a child to become overly self-conscious, so that they question everything they engage in. They are about periodic check-ins, periodic and sometimes enforced breaks in the service of conversations, self-reflection, alone time with books or non-computerized games, attention to family, meals and quality time in nature.

As with addiction issues generally, the question is one of inner freedom, and the *space between* the addictive stimulus and one's response. This speaks to the whole problem of delay of gratification of course but at a larger level it speaks to a liberation from the chains of polarized thinking and emoting. It speaks to the question of whether or not people will become enslaved to single points of view to the utter exclusion of competing points of view, to narrow identifications, to fetishes (be they devices or routines); or whether people will exercise a degree of will over their involvements, and space for the unknown, the surprising, and the paradoxical. In other words, the question will be to what extent will children learn to live a full and rich life, and draw on that life to whatever it is that calls, be it computations or treatises on world peace?

Nurturing that radiance is key—it is key to lively and dynamic living, and it is key to the dignity and esteem that genuinely lifts a person not apart from, but alongside of, all the trials for which they will labor and to which in the end they will succumb. As the holocaust survivor Viktor Frankl learned, if a ray of light penetrating a barrack in a death camp can be turned into an image of a radiant spouse speaking words of encouragement, then just about any problem can be transformed, cohabitated with, and unchained, with the acquisition of inner freedom—and inner freedom is precisely the counterbalance to mechanization.

The next question is how can that inner freedom, presence, and awe be bolstered at school from the moment a child enters formal training?

Awe-Based Education and High Tech

Just as in childrearing, the awe-based relationship between students and high tech begins with presence. If we can't help students to be present—involved, alive, expressive—then the entire edifice of education becomes an exercise in either rote memorization or appeasing the power brokers of culture. It is the rare student, it seems, who can emerge from this edifice as an engaged, awe-informed inquirer.

Right now, the educational system in the U.S. is geared not toward the cultivation of presence, but toward the cultivation of a wage earner. A wage-earner is important of course, but an awe-inspired, present wage earner is much healthier, both for the individual and those around him or her. Consider, for example, one of the major trends currently dominating the primary and secondary levels of education. This trend is called the Common Core Curriculum (CCC). To be sure, the CCC takes several important steps to advance education and make it more relevant to the current philosophical and practical ethos. On the philosophical side, it emphasizes stronger scientific and critical thinking curricula that help students to become more aware and discerning citizens. It defragments some of the regressive trends in education to teach simplistic bible-based principles, such as creationism, or the literal interpretation of scripture. In so doing it helps to ensure that students from various parts of the country have a shared base of knowledge that is consistent with modern ideas about technology, the treatment of others, and the ideal operation of a democratic society. On the practical side, the CCC aims at the education of job-relevant skills, and functional principles of knowledge. It is in part a response to the drop-off in technical skills, such as computer science and math, which have rendered U.S students inferior to increasing numbers of corresponding students in other industrialized nations. The net result of this appears to be a weakening of our capacity to technologically advance and to keep up with the intensifying demands for technical knowledge. The recent STEM disciplines concept, which presses schools to emphasize *S*cience, *T*echnology, *E*ngineering, and *M*athematics, is a definite byproduct of this aforementioned dilemma.

Related to the above is the growing need among employers for students educated in information technology. With the mounting use of computers as the backbone for diverse systems of social functioning, from infrastructure to transportation to healthcare to national security and beyond, the CCC stresses that informational reading and informational comprehension is central.

That said, there are many concerns associated with the CCC mandate which rarely get the media attention they deserve. The main problem from an awe-based standpoint is that the emphasis on information technologies appears to be far too top-heavy and is squeezing out already sapped arts and humanities curricula, not to mention more experiential types of engagements. The pendulum has swung far too vehemently in the direction of formulaic, linear thinking, and not enough in the direction of personal, embodied experiencing. And this is where we leave students adrift.

In addition, there are far too many students who are discouraged from more awe-based, human service studies because of the pressures of the marketplace for technical and corporate vocations. This trend is bolstered by childrearing and educational practices that forfeit wonder, curiosity and intimate reflections on life for those that are packaged, programmed and businesslike. Many students in my own field of psychotherapy, for example, hunger for fuller, deeper relational encounters, but feel pressed into short-term, technical practices in order to conform to the short-term, technical needs of powerful third party payers, such as healthcare corporations. The students capitulate to these pressures not only to pay off their enormous student loans, but to remain in step with the short-term, quick fix culture within which they were raised, and now—too frequently—trained. Longer-term in depth therapy, which therapeutic research has shown to be optimal for many, is increasingly seen as a luxury by such students, and neglected or eliminated altogether in many psychological and psychiatric training facilities.

These trends not only cut against the grain of a humanitarian society, they stifle well-rounded, academic intelligence and deprive our culture of dynamic and motivated workers, caretakers and leaders. Correspondingly, these problems do not even touch on the bitterness that results from such deprivations, which all too readily leads to hostile and conflicted relationships, narrow political and religious identifications, and ultimately susceptibility to engage in wars.

That said, there is at present a striking opportunity to combine awe-based, humanitarian inquiries with sophisticated, high tech skill-building. But if this collaboration is to happen, it needs to be whole-hearted. It needs to begin at the earliest stages of schooling with the strongest emphases on "whole-bodied" education. For example, it is not enough for children to exercise their muscles or be exposed to natural surroundings once or twice a week; they need to be supported in these activities *every day.* It is not enough to go on field trips to museums or concert halls once a year—such excursions should occur closer to once a month, as should excursions to places well beyond concert halls or museums. Among these, for example, may be visits to historical sites, places of business, and even spiritual and religious settings. Such ventures can ignite students' imaginations and fuel their personal and academic conversations. The idea here would be to inspire inquiry, inspire the possibilities of being alive and of discovering as much as one can about the world. The recent incorporation of meditation into some U.S. primary schools is another example of such whole-bodied discovery. The participation of students in plays, the viewing of evocative films and the engagement of students in festive rituals can also help bring them alive. Such enactments would not only help students to talk about their cultural, historical and scientific curiosities, but to touch, taste and feel them, just as they do with their most absorbing experiences outside of school.

To give an example of how such "awe-based" learning could take place in a more technical field, such as general science, consider a course designed around an excursion to Mars, or another potentially habitable planet. The course could frame the classroom as a spaceship, the teacher as the captain, and the students as passengers with various roles to perform. The teacher could then pose the following kinds of issues over the term of the course: "We are about to embark on a fascinating mission to a planet 100 million miles away—what steps do we need to take to prepare for such a journey? What work roles might we play to facilitate the journey? What kind of spacecraft would we need to design to get there? What equipment will we need along the way? How do we prepare physically and psychologically for such a journey? What kinds of communication will need to take place with ground control to optimize our journey? What conditions can we expect to encounter once we arrive at Mars?" The context of these questions would be riveting—that is space travel to an intriguing destination and each of the questions would be ripe for research and inquiry. Moreover, what an exhilarating way to learn about astronomy, physics, chemistry, psychology, anthropology and even potentially philosophy?

In the education of technical fields specifically, visiting space and aeronautic exhibits, or reading stories as I did about scientific discoveries that transformed the world, we can also supplement formal, disciplined education in those fields. The viewing and reading of science fiction is also a wonderful way to spark students' imaginations about how life on earth could be improved or destroyed, unified or divided, by possible discoveries of mind, interplanetary travel, innovative moral or philosophical beliefs, and dramatic new forms of engineering. Why do quality television shows, such as *Star Trek: The Second Generation, The Outer Limits,* or *Twilight Zone*—or these days *Humans, Westworld,* or even *Black Mirror*—need to be ruled out as stimulants to quality education? What about films like *2001: A Space Odyssey*, Tarkovsky's *Solaris, Ex Machina* or scores of other excursions into the unknown?

When students study one-celled organisms or plant life, why not take them to nearby ponds or parks? Instruct them about collecting samples in the wild not just the school lab. When students investigate computing, why not escort them to a high-tech company that builds computer parts or that uses computers to run equipment or to enhance social media? Why not have people who are passionate about their work conduct the tours with these students, talk to the students about their fears and fantasies regarding particular careers, and convey to them the basis for the tour guide's own on-the-job interests/passions?

Morality and High Tech

I suggest an entirely new course or set of courses focused on the moral uses of technology. This curriculum would help students to explore the awe-based possibilities for a variety of future encounters with technology. For example, one theme in such a course could center on the morality of start-up companies, and pose questions for students about the kinds of start-ups they might fantasize about, how those start-ups would treat their workers, how and to what extent they would serve their surrounding community and the world at large, what the start-up might mean to the student(s) personally, and how their personal vision may impact the lives of those served? Also, can a start-up in high tech serve psychological or spiritual needs for physical or social well-being? Instead of framing start-up activity in the context of instant banking or simplistic forms of entertainment such as ease of shopping or net surfing, perhaps students could be asked about the prospects of their start-up to serve the needs of the indigent, alleviate disease or "green" the environment. What about start-ups supporting the aged, making knowledge and technology more readily available to underprivileged youth, as some leaders in the high-tech industry have already done, but now on a much greater scale? Or what of the capacity for start-ups to provide work opportunities to rebuild the nation's infrastructure—roads, bridges, mass transit, etc.? There are a wide range of motivations that could be explored, challenged and discussed in such a class, and an equally wide range of observations made about how given start-ups could improve people's emotional, spiritual and creative lives, as well as, or even as alternatives to, their drive for profit or material gain. This is one facet of engagement with the humility and wonder or sense of adventure toward living.

Many other questions could be posed in a morality and high tech course, such as the role of morality in urban design, aesthetics and community relations. Alternatively, the question could be posed: "If you were to run a modern American city, how would you use high tech?" "What are the various applications of high tech that you personally would find in alignment with your deeply held values, life philosophy or spiritual yearnings?"

There could be discussions about the role of high tech for disabled persons, such as the famous scientist Stephen Hawking whose ALS disease precludes him from eating, speaking and moving in anything remotely close to normal physical functioning. Indeed, the question of "How does a Stephen Hawking manage, and not just manage, but thrive?" would be an extraordinarily rich topic for discussion. Such an inquiry might also bring up the incredible attitude Hawking takes, not just toward the technological world he investigates professionally, but the one he dwells in daily. A related strand here is Hawking's remarkable passion for discovery, for mathematical eloquence, and above all perhaps, for the awesomeness and incomprehensibility of existence itself. Hawking's resonance with the vastness of space and time, the intricacy of star systems and cosmic voids, may well have kept his mentality far above the emotional and physical paralysis that so often typifies his condition. Hawking's refusal to succumb to the narrow identifications of his catastrophic illness and his corresponding delight in the bigger picture of living is a paragon of the awe-based entwinement with the mechanical. And let us not forget the voice-activated computer and automated wheelchair Hawking utilizes as further examples of his awe-based entwinement with the mechanical!

Another potentially fruitful topic might be the speculation about one's interactions with a robot, or even a robot mate, which may not be that far off as a reality. How might one interact with a robot? Can one become intimate with it—what does that even mean? What feelings or thoughts might one have about a robot's role in one's life? Should it be a mechanical assistant, a "friend" as in the British television show *Humans*; a life companion as in the film *Her*? Or should it be treated as a strictly convenient slave as in the film *Ex Machina*—and what might the consequences be of such a treatment, both for the entity and the person? On the other hand, to what extent does one give one's power over to such an entity, and how can such an entity serve rather than squelch awe-based sensibilities? In the aforementioned show *Humans* an attractive robot, or "synth" as she's called, actually kisses a live human being. Can metal and electrical circuitry inspire flesh? And if so at what cost, gain?

How can the sense of awe, which again promotes ambiguous, paradoxical life experiences, mesh with powers to genetically engineer fetuses, erase painful memories or engage virtual realities? Can the sense of awe in nature or face-to-face relationships coincide with or perhaps even complement the sense of awe in virtual communications, virtual travel, and computerized access to knowledge? Can the sense of awe, as distinct from the military's notion of "shock and awe," coexist with weaponry, the use of drones and contrasting views of morality? These latter questions may be the most difficult to reconcile but could, at the same time, be the most evocative in terms of *how technology is used* as distinct from how it may "use" or entrance us. For example, I can think of a place where weaponry may be compatible with moral awe when it comes to the self-defense of our planet from say a meteor attack, or as a last resort to prevent individual or collective annihilation. However, these are precisely the kinds of issues that a course on morality and high tech would inevitably broach—both as a hedge against oversimplification and as a caution about power.

Awe and the Technology of Work

The bedrocks for awe-based work are awe-based childrearing and education. Awe-based work is the humility and wonder, sense of adventure toward specific work tasks as well as overall work vision. The question is how the awe-based experiences of childrearing and education inform the routines, strategies and technologies of contemporary work; or to put it another way, to what extent can the routines, strategies and technologies of work become animated through awe?

While there are obviously no blanket answers to this question, we can surmise that with backgrounds inspired by awe, workers would endeavor to translate the yearnings and reveries of their youth. That is, many workers would bring a profound appreciation for life to the work setting. They would appropriate this appreciation to themselves as well as to those with whom they interact. They would bring an attitude of discovery, reflectiveness and depth to whomever and whatever they engaged with. They would have the desire to bring their workplaces alive, to make them, to the extent possible, laboratories for experimentation and the enhancement of product quality not just profitability or quantity. They would experience a concern for community, both their own at the worksite and that in the world at large. Co-workers would more likely be seen as "fellow travelers" rather than simply employees or competitors. The attitude among workers would be more in the vein of journeyers assembled around life-affirming tasks.

To this extent, work settings of the future may be designed more like starships as depicted in such films as *Star Trek,* rather than as factories. Whatever it is that workers pursue, be it farming, manufacturing, transportation, provision of medical care, or serving food, the atmosphere that is likely to be fostered is one of "how can this production become a personal and interpersonal project rather than simply a means to a commercial end?" "How can work become an adventure into the unknown and uncharted, alongside the known and reliable?" When technology is approached in these ways, it becomes the servant of something higher and broader. It becomes the instrument of evolutionary growth both for the individual worker and the community for which that worker serves.

Such an awe-based approach, however, would probably require some fundamental changes in how work is conducted and for whom. The more that work can become a worker-owned, collaborative project, the greater the chance that employees will feel empowered. The more that employees feel empowered, the greater the likelihood that they will pursue socially and spiritually meaningful aims. If such an approach is complemented by monthly reflections on the quality and purpose of the work, then there is an even greater likelihood for social and spiritual evolution. If the questions are posed, what really *matters* about the task one performs and what energy is one *willing* to bring to make the task matter?, there is likely to be a very different atmosphere both within and outside of job sites as they are currently constituted.

As with childrearing and education, the cultivation of the sense of discovery and the appreciation for life, are likely to become prime values in the framing and conduct of work. But instead of merely inquiring into those values, this workplace vision would *foster* them in the practical world. Hence, the childhood conjectures about the role of profit, technology and ethics in an awe-based sense of life, would now be put to the "real-world" test. Some issues might be, how are you willing to treat fellow workers? In what ways will you serve society, impact the environment and contribute to the welfare of humanity? Will money be your bottom line, or a means to enhance the personal and social conditions within which you live? How will you define those personal and social conditions, by the measuring stick of material gain, or by the criteria of personal and interpersonal fulfillment? What kind of products would you be willing to produce—those which fuel short-term, but destructive ends, such as fast food, cigarettes and weaponry, or longer-term, life-enhancing ends, such as the promotion of emotional and physical well-being?

These are not mere pipe dreams, but realities that are already seeding the work world. In contemporary worker-owned businesses for example, more and more employees are asking questions about the value of their industry to each individual employee, to the communities they serve, and to the planet as a whole. Worker-owned businesses are burgeoning and have now surpassed private sector unions in population (over 12 million employees nationwide). Most of the worker-owned businesses in the U.S. entail employee stock ownership to varying degrees. On the other hand, cooperatives, where workers have equal say in the control of their businesses are now an emerging phenomenon. Ohio Solar Cooperative, Evergreen Cooperative Laundry and Green City Growers Cooperative are three examples of successful worker owned businesses in the Cleveland area. The worker owned mega-company called Mondragon in Spain is a paragon for many smaller worker-owned businesses across the globe.[5]

---

[5] Regarding worker owned businesses, see J. Hollander's "The rise of shared ownership and the fall of business as usual." *Fast Company* Newsletter, June 27, 2011. Retrieved

Beyond these beginnings, however, a wide array of awe-based job opportunities could await the young. Inspired by awe-based childrearing and education, such opportunities could become plentiful, and eventually predominate the job market. Imagine, if you will, a job market rife with "higher causes" from sustainability of the environment to the enhancement of emotional and physical health; and from the beautification of urban architecture to the improvement of affordable foods. Just consider the difference between the present and typical employee's response to work as a "paycheck" and a future employee's response to work as a service to something greater, higher and more communal. It is likely, for example, that the baker in a worker-owned "green" cooperative with state of the art equipment will put notably greater care, creativity and energy into his product than the man who is burdened by "top-down" management, indifference to environmental and communal sustainability, and minimally effective equipment. This scenario is also an example of how awe-based attitudes can find synchrony with high-tech infrastructure. To the extent that one's vocational mission is one of discovery, craftsmanship and the enhancement of communal well-being, one's technical implements become means to a vision rather than ends to the daily grind of work.

Similar points could be made about an array of emerging jobs. The writer who uses her computer in the service of consciousness raising, or the salesman who relies on his iPad for a life-affirming and ethical product, are also examples of where high tech and awe can coalesce. Indeed, at some future point, high tech will enable human beings to attain enormous freedoms in their quest for furthering and deepening their imaginations, sensitivities and care for existence as a whole.

But in order for these changes to happen, the entire socio-economic system must be reformed. And this reformation would follow awe-based childrearing and education quite naturally. As appreciation for life becomes more and more of an ethic, the objective of unlimited acquisition of things is likely to fade, and as the obsession with things fades, the rewards and riches of contributing to planetary well-being are likely to escalate. Indeed, the sense of awe in some preliminary studies shows precisely these trends. In one study at the Stanford business school, subjects who were primed to experience the sense of awe reported significantly stronger scores on tests of life satisfaction, patience, and desire for volunteerism than subjects who were primed

---

1/30/17 at https://www.fastcompany.com/1762938/rise-shared-ownership-and-fall-business-usual

for "happiness" or not primed at all.[6] Hence, what we are likely to move toward here is a society that works not just for one's material gain, but for the enjoyment of participating in the material and spiritual gain of communities as a whole, as well as in gains for people of diverse circumstances as a whole. A social contract will emerge that supports the uplift of the collective as well as the individual, and interestingly, technology is likely to play a remarkable role in that transformation. For this would be a time when technology will provide basic comforts and perform the jobs that people would avert, thus freeing people to focus on their larger visions of individual and collective discovery, adventure and creativity. Moreover, there could be concerted time at work to reflect on these priorities, such as the provision of weekly meetings to discuss the meaning and purpose of one's job, one's social vision, and hopes for one's vocational future. Such meetings would be voluntary and could be facilitated by experts in group process.

Who would pay for all these reforms? The same people who are paying now to create socially responsible companies, long-term investments in their communities and rejuvenation of the environment. In addition, however, the awe-based companies of the future will be comprised of many more people; people who are disposed toward conscientiousness from the outset, and who participate in cultures that value lives over profits. Such people will also populate boards, legislatures and governments that prioritize opportunities for meaningful work and that delimit the monopolization of wealth. While these ideas may seem ludicrous in many quarters of the business world today, I believe they will be eminently logical in the business world of tomorrow—particularly if that world is infused with veneration for life, humility toward existence and fascination with discovery.

Awe and the Science and Technology Sector

The question here would be how can the sense of awe animate jobs in science and technology? Einstein brilliantly set the table for this challenge when he wrote:

The most beautiful thing we can experience is the mysterious.

---

[6] The link among awe, life satisfaction, patience and volunteerism is from M. Rudd, K.D. Vohs, & J. Aaker's "Awe Expands People's Perception of Time, Alters Decision Making, and Enhances Well-Being," *Psychological Science, 23,* 1130–1136, 2012. doi: 10.1177/0956797612438731.

It is the source of all true art and science. He to whom the emotion is a stranger, who can no longer pause to wonder and stand wrapped in awe, is as good as dead—his eyes are closed. The insight into the mystery of life, coupled though it be with fear, has also given rise to religion. To know that what is impenetrable to us really exists, manifesting itself as the highest wisdom and the most radiant beauty, which our dull faculties can comprehend only in their most primitive forms— this knowledge, this feeling is at the center of true religiousness.[7]

To be sure, not every engineering or biotechnology task could be approached with Einstein's vigor of feeling, but many can and should. First of all, employees entering these fields will already have had substantial immersion in the arts and humanities, in experiential learning and field trips, in quality science fiction, and in big questions about morality. Even time taken to appreciate the marvels of bridge design, civic architecture, computer wizardry and the experimental method would be time well spent. This approach is also where some kind of contemplative period could help workers to become more fully present in their jobs, and to apprehend those jobs within a larger context of purpose, meaning, awe. The rub here is to help employees feel, not just think about, how their biological samples, or computer designs, or algorithmic calculations fit into a larger picture of care for their fellow humans and the planet as a whole. Such a perspective would also help employees turn on to the specialty they have chosen— its unending possibilities, variety of applications and potential for life enhancement.

Awe, High Tech, and Religiosity

Religious and spiritual engagements can play pivotal roles in the awe-based transformation of societies. To the extent that religious and spiritual engagements emphasize the awesomeness of life, they will help reinforce the awe-based developments of childrearing, education and work. Indeed, I propose that "awe-based spirituality" infuse the philosophy and practice of religion. As a base for considering one's

---

[7] The quote from Einstein on "the mysterious" is from Walter Isaacson's *Einstein: His Life and Universe* (New York: Simon & Schuster, 2007, p. 387).

relationship to existence, isn't it time for the world to embrace such a sensibility?

One approach to awe-based spirituality could be the respectful incorporation of the world's major religions within each of those religions. By this I mean some form of interchanging services within each of the major houses of worship. Hence, a Buddhist service could be invited by a Catholic priest, or a Hindu ritual could be requested by a Jewish rabbi, or a Taoist sermon could be sought after by a Muslim mullah and so on, followed by a discussion period. The idea here would be to share in the cross-cultural riches of awe-based spirituality integral to each of the great traditions, and thereby deepen and expand the awe-based spirituality of individual heritages.

Variations of this approach have already been tried of course at a handful of interfaith and more traditionally-based religious settings. That which hasn't been tried to my knowledge is the more radical step of integrating rotating services and congregations into the philosophies and actual precepts of the religions. Now although this may sound outlandish from the standpoint of traditional religions, I think it can be looked at much more seriously when we consider the *essential* aspects of each of those religions. For example, they all converge on the valuing of human life, although the emphases on the so-called afterlife may differ; they all prize tolerance and even appreciation for fellow human beings, be they strangers or nonbelievers; they all foster humility before the vastness of creation or God; and they all stress mercy or compassion for the poor or underprivileged. While I realize that there are many nuances and details on which these aforementioned traditions differ, there is nevertheless a core that is common to all; and except for the most doctrinaire, this core is awe-based. The question is, can we tap this core for the good of humanity?

The answer of course is complex; for there are many questions— both personal and practical—about how such an awe-based process would be received. For example, some people would object to the idea that their traditional services may be watered down, or that creeds foreign to them may offend. How could a Jewish congregant for instance sit idly by while Jesus, with all the historical loading thereby implied, is proclaimed as his savior; or a Buddhist sit calmly before Muslim declarations about martyrdom in the name of Muhammad; or a Muslim stand receptively before Christian exultations about the rapture; or a Hindu witness peaceably Jewish chants about being the chosen people; and so on?

Nothing would be easy about these stances, but they are doable and more importantly imperative if we are to crack the barriers of fear and hatred that beset contemporary communities. One path to such stances is hinted at, ironically, by the secular revolution begun by Freud. This revolution demonstrated that nonrational subliminal fears coexist with those that are conscious and rational; and that furthermore we can "treat" or work with those nonrational realms so that they can be integrated into, and even enrich, everyday living. That is, we can learn to live with and thrive from the contrasting and contradictory impulse within. And one of the first ways we can cultivate this sensibility is through the recognition that just about everything we dread is within ourselves, as well as those toward whom we project our dreads. Indeed, it is chiefly through the contradictory that we learn the more of who we are and develop increased abilities to get along with ourselves and others, see the world from more angles, and create lifestyles, communities, and artistic and spiritual expressions that deepen our experience of living.

The question is how do we cultivate the abilities to hold these varying perspectives and still remain cohesive as a person, with deeply held values, a heritage, and a religious or spiritual direction? The accumulated wisdom of psychotherapy in many forms tells us that it is through presence—the capacity to hold and illuminate that which is palpably significant within ourselves and between ourselves and others—that we can preserve both individuality *and* communalism. Furthermore, it is precisely this presence, this coexistence with the contradictory, that awe-based childrearing, education and work would teach us, and hence transfer to our religious and spiritual lives. To the extent that congregants of all creeds then can cultivate presence, they will also be able to encounter and integrate the seemingly disparate ideologies of heritages foreign to them. To the extent that congregants, or just plain spiritual seekers, can cultivate presence, the chief aspirations of the major religions will be fulfilled. Among these aspirations are the development of loving, appreciative and awe-inspired lives; lives that matter and lives that grow. Correspondingly, the chief aspirations of many secular traditions would likewise be fulfilled. Such trends are already evident as more and more religious seekers recognize these dimensions, and are considered the fastest growing religious demographic in the United States. These seekers are euphemistically called "Nones," which refers roughly to nonaligned explorers of spiritual and religious enlightenment.[8] At the same time, there are also increasing numbers of religious devotees who see the value of interfaith encounters, and hence the rise of such encounters in more liberal and awe-based organizations. People are increasingly recognizing that they can be both centered in their particular heritage *and* enlightened, enlivened or even inspired by the beauty of other heritages, particularly when the elements of humility and wonder or sense of adventure toward living can be shared and integrated.

What has all this to do with high tech? In our rapidly industrializing world, a great deal. Despite the rise in convergence between religious and secular worlds as illustrated by the Nones, there is an equal if not more virulent separation between these worlds. But it needn't continue this way. In fact, what needs to happen is to carry forth the revolutions of Kierkegaard, Nietzsche and Freud in recognizing a more holistic portrait of humanity. This portrait would delimit the influence of rationalism, or the machine model for living, and expand the influence of depth psychology, mind/body synchrony and paradoxical living. The tent of religiosity, as distinct from doctrinaire religion, is wide enough to encompass the awe-inspired scientist as well as the God-inspired worshiper, the atheist as well as the believer, and the skeptic as well as the reverent. This is because it is neither doctrines nor analyses that fire the religious/spiritual yearning, but rather the whole-bodied experience of life. It is the whole-bodied experience of life that leads to stirring questions about the nature of the universe, the complexity of living organisms and the enigma of death. It is the whole-bodied experience of life that stirs us before the monuments of history, the marvels of science, and the depth, grace and beauty of art.

Accordingly, can we not also provide a contemplative space—within our religions—for awe-based science and art? Might we add to our services contemplations about what inspires the painter, the photographer or the sculptor; or the writer, the poet or the performer? Or by the same token, could we make space for the awe-based testimonies of the scientist concerning DNA sequencing, or the neurologist concerning neural circuitry, or the engineer regarding bridge design, and so on? For these attestations too are arguably religious and would have a place in the awe-based service of the future.

If I were to partake in such an awe-based service, I would share my experience at Columbia University where I taught a couple of

---

[8] For a discussion of the "Nones," see E. Weiner's "Americans: Undecided About God?" *The New York Times* Sunday Review, December 11, 2011.

summer sessions.[9] From the physical environment to the libraries, this was a "religious" experience for me. Here is an entry from my diary upon first entering the place in 2012—and it contains both rational and nonrational dimensions:

> My first feeling upon entering the gates of the university is that it took 56 years to get here, and finally I've arrived! My father enrolled in an education workshop here in the late '50s and I still have body memories of that journey. In particular I remember the dark brick buildings I passed as my mother wheeled me up and down Broadway in a baby carriage while my father was in class. I am also acutely aware that my father was born and raised in New York City and that I spent many a summer (quite literally!) bathing in its majesty.
>
> My second feeling as I stood on the quad was an observation of a building on my right that had the following inscriptions in bold letters—'Socrates, Plato, Aristotle, Demosthenes and Vergil,' among a few others, and I knew that I was 'home.' It felt like this was ground zero for some great American presence of Western (Hellenic) culture. Then I had the feeling that this was the august Butler Library, which I had just read about in a glowing tribute in *The New York Times* on my flight over to New York. So here I was having this religious feeling over philosophers and libraries!
>
> Next, I ascended the copious steps of the other grand building on the quad, Low Memorial Library. As I entered the foyer, I felt pulled to another grand room, a rotunda just to my right. The rotunda turned out to be an enormous auditorium that looked like an 18th century version of a medieval cathedral, except it was secular! Truly, the room felt like a cathedral of Hellenic knowledge, and I even observed a patron in the room kneeling as if in prostration before the solemn visage. That visage, lined with the busts of revered scholars, displayed the words 'Law' on the left and 'Philosophy' on the right, and again I knew that I had arrived home in some profound sense. I felt home in the sense that I imagined some medieval pilgrim might have felt at the first sight of Notre Dame or Chartres in Paris—

[9] My abiding appreciation goes to Teachers College, Columbia University Clinical Psychology faculty Lisa Miller, Barry Farber, and Aurelie Athan for their support and graciousness during my visiting lectureships.

except this was a shrine dedicated to democratic values of inquiry, reason and imagination.

Why can't there be an equal reverence for the so-called secular, I thought, which can be just as cosmic, wondrous and stirring as the great shrines and monuments of religion? Why couldn't I sense the same (or similar) trepidation, chill and thrill in my bones as the medieval pilgrim 10 centuries past (or for that matter, present)? For here at Low Library, was in my view, the U.S. equivalent of Notre Dame—except that the solemnity and veneration were for the glory of human achievement *in the context of cosmic possibility* as distinct from the preconceived possibilities of a biblical God. Not that such a God could not exist, but I would wager that if it does exist, there would be much more to appreciate than a set of commands or a definable entity. What I experienced at Low, what really thrilled me, was the glory of the universe without the presumption of an Overseer; the sense of zeal without a preconceived Truth (precisely in lieu of such a Truth!).

The only similar experience I had was during a visit to the University of Vienna. I had just returned from a conference and a very personable colleague, Alfried Langle, was gracious enough to give me a tour of the university. The first things that struck me upon entering the main hallway were a sense of solemnity and depth. It seemed to me that the place was imbued with genius. I can't explain it exactly but it was palpable—so many great minds, so many pioneering hearts, so much seriousness about life and the living process. Then as I walked down the hallway I witnessed the busts of great mentors past— a few of them I recognized from my philosophy courses, such as Franz Brentano and Karl Popper. Also, Moritz Schlick who was assassinated at the university by a young fascist in 1936 and for whom there is a plaque at the very spot of his demise. Then of course, there was a bust of Sigmund Freud, and the actual room where Freud delivered his lectures on hysteria. But none of these 'mementos' could explain the surge of my feeling. It was just a profound sense of awe, of connection, and of being on hallowed ground.

I imagine that many people have their own stories, such as the engineer who marvels at bridge design, or the pianist who stammers before the melodies of a Beethoven sonata, or the soccer player who feels transported following a successful goal.

> These experiences are comparable to and cannot, to my mind, be separated from profound experiences of liturgy."

Given such circumstances, why should houses of worship be confined to sectarian ceremonies? Why can't they also be places for people to share diversified experiences of the sacred from varied walks of life? To be sure, such interchanges might also include that which has traditionally been called the secular, such as the rational, the scientific and the technological, but they need not be for secular ends, such as instruction or edification. Within the context of religiosity, by contrast, they would be for communal ends, communal discoveries and communal deepenings of our common spiritual heritage.

The opening to this expansion of religiosity brings another question to mind: how would it be facilitated and within what denominational boundaries? It is one thing for example for people to discuss their sacral experiences of music or architecture during a group contemplation, but it is quite another for them to discuss their sacral experiences of lovemaking or fighting or any of a range of idiosyncratic and potentially disturbing events. Where is the line for a given denomination, and who is to draw it? While there may be no hard and fast lines in such an awe-based culture, and respect would be core to the ethos, surely there will be challenges to the given denomination, as well as given individuals within denominations that would demand deft and concerted management. This is the point at which I would advocate another bold reform within the traditional framework of religiosity— *the training of clergy in the depth psychology of group process.*

My point here is that challenges such as those noted above happen all the time in therapeutic group settings, and they are skillfully managed in a majority of circumstances. But they are skillfully managed because the facilitators of such groups have backgrounds in group and individual psychology, and the deeper their backgrounds in these areas, the more likely their facilitations will be effective.[10] The same principle applies, it seems to me, to clergy, or to any of a range of depth facilitators. The more such leaders can become sensitized to and help manage problematic transactions, the sturdier their group experiences are likely to be. Correspondingly, the more that such leaders become

---

[10] By "deeper" I mean possessing the personal and interpersonal skills of therapeutic empathy, alliance, collaboration, moment-to-moment attunement, etc. that I noted earlier (e.g., Elkins' *The Human Elements of Therapy*) and which are strongly associated with therapeutic effectiveness.

psychospiritually adept, the richer and more rewarding their overall facilitations are likely to be.

To be clear, this suggestion is not aimed at converting religious/spiritual groups into psychotherapy groups, but to *sensitizing* socially and spiritually significant leaders to matters that cross spiritual, religious and therapeutic bounds; and to strengthen those leaders to optimally support their respective group contexts.

What depth psychology gives us then is a fuller picture of the contrasting and contradictory impulses of the person. It debunks the illusions of both rationalist philosophy and doctrinaire religion, for instance, that all will be well and all can be fixed through God, logic or formulae. Yet, what depth psychology and anthropology have shown is that all has not been well under these dogmas. Indeed much has been disastrous—from antiquity through the mass destruction of the 20th and 21st centuries.

The upshot of these observations is that now is the time for a new religiosity. This is a religiosity that opens to the inquiries of science as well as to raptures of religious traditions; that invites the atheist and theist to revel together; and the Christian, Muslim, Jew, Hindu, Buddhist, Taoist, Sikhist, Goddess worshiper, Paganist, Ubuntuist and Shintoist to sit together, speak with one another, and discover from one another the essence of their teachings. Then and only then will we know religiosity at its core; its aspiring height.

Awe, Technology and Government

The legislative process in many industrialized countries is disabled. It seems that "voting one's conscience," a core of the democratic spirit of deliberation, has too often given way to voting to stay elected, or to appease vested interests, or to attain the "quick fix"—and the results have been all too apparent.

To this extent, the legislative process in the industrialized world has fallen victim to the same kinds of social and economic forces that have blunted vitality in that world generally—the machine model for living. As indicated previously, the machine model for living emphasizes speed, instant results and image over substance. It's not that deliberative, substantial forms of legislation have never been forged, quite to the contrary, as civil rights, worker rights, food and drug regulation, and many other forms of social support have attested. However, in the past couple of decades and particularly in the United States, this deliberative and substantive approach has eroded. As political polarization and cronyism has grown, major psychospiritual reforms have nosedived. Among these reforms are greater access to quality education, increased opportunities for personally meaningful work, increased access to longer term, in depth mental health services, and greater devotion to intercultural exchange and peacebuilding. Moreover, this stalemate has given way to the powerful influences of big corporations and a tiny percentage of billionaires who generally get their way. Corporate and financial influence have "bought" many of the legislators while alienating many others; but these others have become increasingly powerless and in order for them to stay in office they must compromise to the tune of a desiccated middle class, a bloated military, a deregulated financial sector and a growing underclass. Each of these developments has brought the United States to the brink of disaster through preemptive wars, fabricated coups, the crack up of Wall Street, and the crumbling of social support systems.

That said, if we think these issues are problematic, it is almost incalculable to conceive how the power elite will approach the tools of transhumanism. Will such tools—nanotechnology, genetic engineering, robotics, artificial intelligence and the like be approached with the same zeal for profit, material gain, and military power for which many former technologies have been utilized? Will such "instruments" be used to manipulate consumers to enrich the pockets of a few, while relegating the moral and ethical fallout to a haphazard and indifferent marketplace?

It is in this light that several years ago, I was spurred to embark on an ambitious project: to translate awe-based principles of presence, freedom, courage and appreciation to the legislative arena (see also Martin Buber's idea of "I and Thou" dialogue). The core idea of this "Experiential Democracy Project," as I call it, is to supplement the bureaucratically-heavy legislative system with a personal or "experiential" component that should, in theory, provide a check on what is now a very routinized, and too often one-dimensional process.

Experientially-based deliberation, or "experiential democracy" for short, is a "here and now," personally-oriented supplement to standardized legislative proceeding. Put another way, it is an opportunity for intensive reflection about an issue of moral import— such as the place of military intervention, or as will be illustrated later, the experience of community policing—and for the maximization of consensus through empathy. Experiential deliberation is not intended to dominate but to supplement communal and governmental decision making; it is an attempt to ensure integrity, both within and among deliberators. The following is a brief overview of how an experientially-based legislative proceeding might work:

> Two diversely opinionated legislators who are members of the same legislative committee would agree to participate in four expertly facilitated and confidential meetings over a one-month period, possibly accompanied by one or two legislator observers from the same panel. In this media-free meeting, the depth psychological facilitator would present the legislators with one or two morally significant, currently active agenda items that have been agreed to in advance.

The meeting would provide a forum for mindful turn-taking in which each legislator would briefly offer his or her personal and heartfelt perspective on the selected agenda item. The opposing legislator would then be asked to reflect back on what they had just heard, and the counterpart would have a chance to correct any misunderstanding. Afterwards, the roles would be reversed. The interaction would then proceed to a deepening or elaboration of the thoughts and feelings that emerged from this process of mutual disclosure. In particular, each party would be asked to declare the important meanings or understandings that the dialogue had produced, and how or whether their opinions of the legislation had changed as a result.

Finally, each legislator would consider whether an identifiable consensus had been achieved, or what steps would be needed to achieve consensus. A recording secretary or observer would then summarize the deliberations and prepare a written report that focuses solely on conclusions about the specific agenda item and that strictly excludes the disclosure of any personal information about the thoughts or emotions expressed by either party. This report would then be brought to the entire legislative committee for general discussion and integration into further deliberative proceedings. In addition, a brief assessment at the end of the four sessions could be used to help determine the utility and viability of the proposed procedure.

It seems to me that there is a new readiness, and perhaps even hunger, among constituents for a substantive check on the present mode of political decision making. I believe we can foster a new dimension in the legislative deliberation process that emphasizes an in depth, personal component in conjunction with, and as a supplement to, the conventional group deliberation that has prevailed. This would be a natural "next step" in the deepening and enrichment of the democratic process envisioned by our forebears. I therefore hope that experiments like this in experiential democracy might be initially tried on a small and carefully monitored scale throughout the country, with data collected and pooled to determine their effectiveness.

Would experiential democracy resolve the problem of profit-or corporate-driven influence on government? Would it balance the scales between technological innovation and public welfare? Probably not. But what experiential democracy is likely to accomplish is a significant reduction in these aforementioned problems. Further, it would promote the mass education needed for people to substantively reflect on and potentially achieve consensus concerning the radical transformations of humanity. These transformations would include everything from the role of robotics in everyday life to "designer" babies to the artificial replacement of body parts, particularly the brain, to the effects of mind-altering drugs to the technologizing of education and the workplace, to the military uses of nanotechnology to the mechanical extension of life. These challenges will, of course, not only involve the deliberations of regulatory bodies, but a broadly educated populace, which is again why it is so crucial for regulatory bodies to start the conversations and provide critical information and/or policy guidelines.

Chapter 6

How an Awe-Based Society Might Look:
The Depth Approach to Transhumanism

While there are many forms of society that have been forged throughout history, rare indeed is the attempt to structure them as "awe-based." For example, we have seen societies based on religious and political ideology—e.g., Christianity and Islam, communism and capitalism, and also societies based on utopian ideals such as transcendentalism, cooperative farming and environmentalism. But how many, particularly large-scale societies, have been formed around the humility, wonder and sense of adventure toward living? How many have prized the commingling of thrill and anxiety for living, or for the capacity to be deeply moved as the cornerstones of their world views?

I think we'd have to acknowledge, very few. And yet this is precisely the kind of society, and world, I believe that we will need to pursue if we are to avoid a transhumanist apocalypse. And we will need to pursue it on a formidable scale.

The reformation of childrearing, the work setting, the religious and spiritual settings, and governance, are fundamental starting points in the reorientation to an awe-based world. The equally large issue however is who or what is going to guide us in this reformation and counterbalance, and how will that guidance begin?

One prospect that has empirical support is a depth psychological approach. By "depth psychological approach" I mean the intimate, "experience-near" understanding of subliminal and symbolic consciousness and its practical applications. This approach is informed by a variety of fields in the social sciences, the arts and the humanities, but is probably best understood as a holistic approach to life.[1] Such an approach has many personal and social advantages that are just now emerging into the mainstream consciousness. One of the primary

---

[1] See *The Polarized Mind* for an elaboration on the holistic-existential dimensions of "depth psychology."

advantages is that it specializes in the cultivation of relationships, and in particular, relationships that support, that hold contrasts and contradictions, and that sensitively challenge as situations demand. To this extent, depth psychology, particularly through it's chief therapeutic tool of presence, appreciates the paradoxes of living, the great vulnerabilities as well as possibilities for living, and the potential for a sense of awe toward all creation.

Further, it is important to note that this depth perspective overlaps with, but also significantly differs from, conventional psychological approaches. For example, whereas depth psychology stresses experiential engagement—that is, the immediate, affective, kinesthetic, and profound—in confronting personal and social conflicts, conventional psychology stresses more cerebral, technical engagement with such conflicts (e.g., the difference between learning *about* change mechanisms of depression, and the *felt discovery* of how depression transforms). Moreover, whereas the conventional approach is more external, mathematically measurable, and based on aggregated research, the depth approach is more internal, qualitatively describable, and based on the intimate experience of individuals. Finally, while the conventional approach advocates the reconditioning of overt and measurable symptoms, such as improvements in positive self-talk, eating and sleeping, the depth approach fosters the self-discovered contexts underlying the symptoms such as the enlargement of one's identity, the enhancement of one's capacity for choice and the reconnection with a bigger picture of living. This picture can include everything from the enhancement of purpose and meaning to the awakening of awe. While both the conventional and depth approaches pertain to given personal or interpersonal needs, the issue here is one of rebalancing the scales—the recognition of depth as a complement to metrics.

Prizing Awe on a Par with Technology

Imagine that for every public school requirement for science, math and computerization, there were an equivalent requirement for art, literature and depth psychology. Imagine that by students' senior year in high school, a curriculum on depth psychology would be seen to be as paramount as a curriculum on human physiology. Again, I am not speaking of a replacement for traditional subjects such as human physiology, but of a reapportionment that is reflective of the needs of an emerging mindset. Such a reapportionment should then carry over to the freshman year of college where literature, humanities and depth psychology would share an equal percentage of the requirements as that for STEM disciplines.

Would such a shift mean that business and biotech majors, computer and engineering students, will be "cheated" out of an optimal education? Would neurosurgery residents and brokerage apprentices be kept from learning the very latest their fields have to offer? In short, would the degree of sophistication called for by many of the specializations today be compromised by a depth psychology/therapy renaissance?

The answer of course depends on whether one feels the compromise is worth it; whether a reprioritization from an efficiency model of living to an awe-based, holistic framework is worth the effort—I feel strongly that it is. To be clear, however, I am not advocating the eradication of specializations, nor am I supporting the sacrifice of essential technical knowledge. That which I am speaking of here is the integration of depth psychology/therapy principles both prior to and during specialized training. I am speaking about engineers having time to appreciate the beauty as well as moral implications of their creations; about medical doctors being supported to improve the art of self-care, as well as care for the holistic experiences of their patients; about financiers being encouraged to reflect broadly on the personal and ethical implications of their investments; and about law enforcement officials being nudged to enhance their deliberative capacities for dialogue, perspective-taking and cultural context. Such supplements to the present focus on specializations may of course require extended periods of study. But if the depth perspectives are integrated proportionally throughout a student's tenure, I suspect that the extensions can probably be limited to a year, which may actually help rather than hinder a student's sense of well-being over the course of his or her training.

I am also speaking here about a reformation of socio-economic ethics. To the extent that a significant percentage of education is devoted to the ideal of profit-making beyond what is reasonably necessary, comfortable and socially equitable, we have forfeited education to something other than the maturation of hearts and minds. This forfeit can be seen today in the wildly disproportionate profits of corporate executives relative to their workers, and the billionaires who represent one percent of the population but who own virtually tax-free more than 50 percent of the world's wealth. Yet, the enlivening, enriching and ethically sensitizing depth studies would be a formidable counter to this skewed mentality. These depth studies, along with the awe-based backgrounds of students in other realms of their lives should all result in major shifts of mentality toward how money is made, who benefits from it, and where spending it is prioritized. My guess is that in the United States this shift in mentality would organically lead to increasing forms of socially responsible investments, worker-owned industries, and personally and socially meaningful jobs. It would also likely lead to a renaissance in the production of environmentally sustainable energy, transportation and agriculture, a more equitable safety net for health and education, and an increased market for socially innovative arts and sciences.

This is a case where machines, ironically, can also play a vital role in the aforementioned transformation. The more that machines advance, the more they can take up roles in the maintenance of our infrastructure—roads, transportation, buildings—the manufacture of a variety of products, and the support of our medical and educational needs. If used mindfully, these forms of assistance can play a critical role in our ability to focus on personally and socially meaningful activity that would otherwise be expended on menial or devitalizing tasks. In this sense, machines can also help us savor more of life, if it is a life we decide to engage in rather than fritter away. This would be a monumental choice to have.

While I realize that machines, or better said, automation, is the chief impediment to job opportunities for individuals in our industrial sectors, this only reinforces my arguments above: the sooner we provide meaningful support and re-specialization training to these struggling workers, the more manageable this industrial transition will be. And the sooner we put a political priority on this automation problem, the sooner we address the demoralization of, and backlash from the core constituencies of the industrialized world.[2]

---

[2] The demoralization of industrial workers due to the displacement of their manufacturing jobs is certainly one of the major factors leading to the election of authoritarian leaders such as Donald Trump. This tone was sounded when Trump proclaimed at his inauguration that "From this day forward, a new vision will govern our land. From this day forward it's going to only be America first." It remains to be seen whether supportive services such as respecialization training, and the identification of automation as the chief long-term challenges to re-employment will be made a priority, beyond the politically expedient though comparatively lesser problem of relocating manufacturing jobs overseas. The quote of Trump is from David Von Drehle's "Trump's American Vision: The New President Reverses Course on a Century of U.S. Leadership," *Time Magazine*, p. 28, January 30, 2017.

The upshot of these observations is that we are dealing with a moral equivalent of war *now*, and need the equivalent of an army of depth facilitators to address this situation. From childrearing to education to work to religious and spiritual settings to government, depth psychological understanding and depth therapeutic facilitators are as essential to the present as engineers, bankers and military officers have been to the past. Depth psychological perspectives are no less vital than the politics, commercial industries and healthcare that we have traditionally depended on for our sustenance. *The emotional infrastructure is as imperative today as the physical infrastructure in years past.* This is because without depth perspectives, a palpable sense of awe, our worlds are about to capsize. We are about to become, if we have not already, the efficient, amoral automatons, and the doleful, embittered souls who perform empty rituals and lifeless routines that our more sensitive forebears feared. While we may smile and revel in a sort of sanitized paradise, underneath many of us are hollow husks— both resentful and devitalized. This is because too often, machines are wresting us from the one trump card we humans hold—the beauty and agony of being alive.

The New Army of Depth Healers

The prizing of awe on a par with technology also means that we have an urgent need for specialists in depth facilitation. It means that in every major sector there is urgency for experts in enriched living. This "army" of depth healers is as important, and hopefully more important, than the conventional army now enshrined; and it must engage in a new war, the war for humanity's dignity. After all, if we're going to have a moral equivalent of war than a "war" indeed is what we will need to wage.

What will the army look like? Perhaps like a public works program for depth facilitation and we can start with a deliberative governmental setting as priority number one. In tandem with the experiential democracy idea proposed earlier, we will need infusions of depth facilitators to work with adversarial legislators, rivaling or even warring diplomats, heads of state and community leaders. Again, these facilitators will not determine policy but they will help to deepen and supplement policy. They will bring an attunement that few (if any?) forms of institutional dialogue currently offer.

The depth army is also needed to bolster the education of teachers. The aim of this supplementation would be to help teachers become more adept at depth exploration—not exploration in the clinical sense, but in the sense of an attunement to students' fuller capacities to mediate conflicts, to engage in sensitive dialogues and to enrich experiential learning. The focus on cultivating presence, on handling blockages to presence and on managing the degrees of intensity of presence, should all be helpful in the acquisition of a variety of student skills. These skills would range from athletics to scientific experimentation to philosophical inquiry.

Such an army would also be invaluable for the public mental health system. Right now, this system is glutted with short-term, symptom-focused treatments. While these treatments tend to pacify, they often do not substantively address desolate lives. To be sure, it's not that a good many professionals in this system fail to perceive its shortcomings—actually a notable number do. But without a sea-change in policy, a reprioritization of government and corporate funding, it is exceedingly difficult to buck the quick fix orientation. Yet this state of affairs is untenable and it will likely grow worse. As long as tax loopholes for the rich and bloated military spending are prized over in depth, publicly accessible relationships, the costs of skyrocketing depression, burgeoning violence and rampant substance abuse are only likely to grow.

An army of depth healers is also needed for the depth dialogues discussed previously in religious and spiritual settings. To the extent that depth facilitators are enabled to enter such settings, they will support religious clergy to foster the intimate, awe-based dialogues previously described. This support is critical in my view because aside from a few courses in pastoral counseling, conventional clergy do not seem adequately trained in depth facilitation of individual and group processes.

A corps of depth facilitators is also badly needed at the worksite, where thousands and perhaps millions are increasingly alienated by mechanized, insular jobs. Such a corps could work with employers and employees to develop "reflection" periods, where say, once a month and on a voluntary basis, professionally facilitated discussion groups could be offered. These groups could bring employees and employers together to reflect on the meaning and implications of their work for themselves, the communities they serve, and the society in which they dwell. The groups moreover could be nurtured by concerted person-to-person dialogues, seminars on holistic health and creativity, reflections on community needs, and considerations of the meanings of particular tasks to the society at large. In short, such groups would provide refreshing opportunities for workers to "step back" and take stock of what it is their doing, how they're doing it, and whether potential reforms could vitalize their collective experience.

Finally, an army of depth facilitators is needed at the level of local governments and even neighborhoods to help resolve disputes, address multicultural tensions and support community activities. Again, these facilitators will not be like ideological "minders" such as we have seen in authoritarian cultures, but open-minded consultants schooled in emotionally attuned, interpersonal mediation.

Where will the funding for this "army" come from? Given that the proposed objective to build our emotional infrastructure is as important as the objective to build roads, bridges and hospitals, I propose a new Public Works Administration on a par with that created in the wake of the Great Depression. This "Public Works Program for Depth Psychology" could be funded by an array of incentives and penalties, from giving tax breaks to those who invest in the program to closing tax loopholes for income earners in the upper one percent, to taxing stock transactions, to taxing companies for hiring overseas. The money could also be diverted from the investment in defunct or wasteful defense contracts. If even a fraction of these monies were available, the Public Works Program for Depth Psychology could begin seeding depth facilitation training tomorrow.

The Intercultural Spirituality of Awe

It should be evident by now that the sense of awe is not only cross-cultural but potentially intercultural, with bridge-building enabling multiple cultures to coexist with and learn from one another. This interweaving can both heal and deepen the human community. Moreover, it can provide support for an expanded human consciousness. To be sure, that consciousness could be a "messy," even contradictory affair; but it could also be profoundly stimulating, energizing, and as suggested earlier, unifying. It would not be unifying in the sense of homogenizing—making everyone alike—but in the sense of appreciating our common human heritage, our search for, cherishing of, and linkage to the beyond.

This whole issue hinges on seeing the "more," or what I have earlier called the "meta-view." It hinges on being able to step outside the box of one's ideology or nationality or race even for one moment, and see a larger view. It is very difficult to do this without training or a facilitator—and yet, on rare occasions we have seen the fruit of such enlarged consciousness, even without a skilled facilitator. For example, in September 1978, Jimmy Carter was ready to leave the peace negotiations between President Sadat of Egypt and Prime Minister Begin of Israel. He and his U.S. entourage all but expected a war in the next month because of the completely stalled negotiations. Sadat and Begin barely spoke with one another for days. But just as it seemed the negotiations were going to completely unravel, Begin asked Carter to sign photographs of the three leaders for his eight grandchildren and Carter obliged with personal notes to each. This event was so moving to Begin—as well as Carter—as they realized more fully the gravity of their meeting, that Begin agreed to stay with the peace talks. Sadat too was apparently quite moved by this sharing of photos, and shared photos of his own grandchildren in response. Eventually, they worked out a compromise with President Sadat that led to a peace treaty that has lasted some 37 years.[3]

Now there are several lessons we can take from this incident that relate directly to awe-based consciousness. The first lesson is the shared reaction toward children. Children seize the heart because they represent the extension of the mystery of human evolution. They represent implications far too vast to capture with intellect, but in photos and touching recollections, they capture a haunting array of associations—even to the most hardened politicians.

The second lesson is that Begin, Carter and Sadat were able to "step outside the box" for a moment and consider the implications of their decision for their families, and by extension the future of humanity. This is how awe-based consciousness can promote "big picture" thinking and feeling that potentially has an impact on many born and unborn lives.

Third, the incident illustrates the creativity of awe-based awareness. Even Carter used this word "creativity" to describe a part of what he felt was necessary to break deadlocks in challenging negotiations. Creativity stems from the ability to see things from different angles and not just the received or traditional ones. By bringing our attention to both the fragility and vastness of our plight as humans, we are inspired to see things from different angles, such as the weight and poignancy of our impact on future generations versus simply tired old politicians or routine policies. Allowing themselves to be shaken, as exhibited by the bond the three leaders' shared over their

---

[3] On the peace talks among Sadat, Begin, and Carter see Jimmy Carter's *Keeping Faith: Memoirs of a President* (Fayetteville, AR: University of Arkansas Press, 1995).

children, led to different ways of thinking about their conflict so that a compromise could be forged.

While it is pure speculation of course, a plausible argument could be made that if depth facilitators had intervened at this summit among U.S., Egyptian and Israeli leaders, the personal dimension of the encounter could well have arisen significantly earlier in the negotiation process than at the desperate "final hour." Although Begin's request for signed photos and the subsequent sharing of photos may not have occurred, it is very likely that other forms of authentic relating and deepening would have led to an earlier consensus and agreement.

Something of this personal interchange also occurred in the concluding moments of the Cuban Missile Crisis in 1962. As I understand it, Premier Khruschchev of the Soviet Union and President Kennedy of the United States were at a complete stalemate tilting toward nuclear catastrophe until Khruschev sent Kennedy a rather rambling and yet heartfelt letter laying out the issues at stake. Here is an excerpt from that October 26 letter:

> Mr. President, I appeal to you to weigh well what the aggressive, piratical actions, which you have declared the USA intends to carry out in international waters, would lead to. You yourself know that any sensible man simply cannot agree with this, cannot recognize your right to such actions.
>
> If you did this as the first step towards the unleashing of war, well then, it is evident that nothing else is left to us but to accept this challenge of yours. If, however, you have not lost your self-control and sensibly conceive what this might lead to, then, Mr. President, we and you ought not now to pull on the ends of the rope in which you have tied the knot of war, because the more the two of us pull, the tighter that knot will be tied. And a moment may come when that knot will be tied so tight that even he who tied it will not have the strength to untie it, and then it will be necessary to cut that knot, and what that would mean is not for me to explain to you, because you yourself understand perfectly of what terrible forces our countries dispose.
>
> Consequently, if there is no intention to tighten that knot and thereby to doom the world to the catastrophe of thermonuclear war, then let us not only relax the forces pulling on the ends of the rope, let us take measures to untie that knot. We are ready for this.

We welcome all forces which stand on positions of peace. Consequently, I expressed gratitude to Mr. Bertrand Russell, too, who manifests alarm and concern for the fate of the world, and I readily responded to the appeal of the Acting Secretary General of the UN, U Thant.

There, Mr. President, are my thoughts, which, if you agreed with them, could put an end to that tense situation which is disturbing all peoples.[4]

This letter seemed to be the opening that in fact Kennedy and his more "cool-headed" advisors had searched for because virtually every other option looked bleak. To further complicate matters, soon after Kennedy received the October 26 letter, on October 27, a U.S. U-2 spy plane was shot down over Cuban airspace, ordered unilaterally by a Soviet lieutenant named Grechko. In the wake of this incident, some of Kennedy's top military advisors advocated an immediate retaliation that could have sparked the doomsday scenario of World War III. Yet, Kennedy rightly surmised that Khruschchev had nothing to do with the order to shoot down the spy plane, and later that day in fact, Khruschchev again wrote Kennedy a letter. This letter conveyed that if the U.S. agreed to dismantle its own missiles in Turkey, and declare so publicly, the Soviets would stand down and withdraw its nuclear arsenal from Cuba. Fortunately, to the exceeding relief of the world, Kennedy chose to ignore many of his advisors, as well as Khruschchev's second letter calling for a public declaration of U.S. withdrawal of missiles from Turkey and responded to Khruschchev's first letter, which was more heartfelt—even invoking the name of the peace-crusading philosopher Bertrand Russel—in its appeal to save humanity. Soon after, accordingly, Kennedy indicated through backchannels, not publicly, that he would withdraw missiles from Turkey, which then resulted in the successful resolution of the crisis.[5]

Again, the question arises, what if a depth facilitator would have engaged the communications between Khruschchev and Kennedy from the start of their relationship—would it have avoided the crisis altogether? Would the very personal qualities that helped resolve the

---

[4] The Kruschchev-Kennedy letter is a quote from the John F. Kennedy Library website. Retrieved January 31, 2017 at http://microsites.jfklibrary.org/cmc/oct26/doc4.html.

[5] The steps leading to the resolution of the Cuban Missile Crisis are also drawn from the John F. Kennedy Library website. Retrieved January 31, 2017 at http://microsites.jfklibrary.org/cmc/oct26/doc4.html.

crisis in its last desperate moments have manifested significantly earlier and with a notably greater margin of safety? Through concerted attention to Khruschchev and Kennedy's own embodied reactions to the crisis, inclusive of their emotions, sensations and symbolic associations, I contend that not only would the crisis have likely been averted in the first place, but many more potential flashpoints between the rivaling adversaries would also have likely been curtailed. There is of course no way to definitively validate these contentions, but what we see both in the case of Khruschchev's letter and Kennedy's solemn contemplation of it suggest that it is personal qualities and profound interpersonal resonance that move moral crises toward resolution, just as it had for Carter, Begin and Sadat.

Today we are faced with enormous political and religious polarizations that regrettably have benefited little from the foreknowledge of personal mediations such as those described above. Moreover, the technological capacities for mass destruction have only grown. I am speaking about the mass annihilation of thousands on September 11, 2001, the subsequent retaliation of a preemptive war in Iraq that compromised hundreds of thousands of lives and radicalized thousands more to ally with the 9/11 terrorists. And now we have extremist factions such as ISIS, Al Qaeda, the Al-Nusra Front in Syria, the Boko Haram in Nigeria, splinter groups in Yemen and Libya, the rising tide of militant nationalism throughout the West and Mid-East, the competition for nuclear weaponry among rogue and radical states, and the list goes on. Most of these upheavals in my view are an understandable consequence of a cycle of polarizations beginning with larger and typically colonial powers squelching smaller and classically nonindustrialized fiefdoms for reasons ranging from imperialism to racism. Moreover, these cycles must be recognized for any substantive stabilization to begin.

On the other hand, there are groups that are so enraged and so bent on vengeance that little but military intervention can stifle their forward momentum. This may be the case with certain groups mentioned above. But the larger and more important point, so often obscured in the drumbeats of war, is that the vast majority of people, as with their leaders, do not want to live under vengeance-based tyrannies; at the very least, they are amenable to dialogue; at most, to substantive treaties. Put simply, these are the people that need to be reached—and not with perfunctory summits or patronizing rhetoric but with awe-based, in depth encounter accompanied by specialized facilitation.

We need to make the kind of desperate breakthroughs of the Kennedy-Khruschchev communications or the Carter-Begin-Sadat summits commonplace diplomacy, and commonplace policies.

The Intercultural Impact of Awe

The beauty of awe is that it can resonate with virtually anyone. One doesn't have to belong to a particular tribe or culture or even religion to be touched by awe. It also affirms people's pain, without resorting to a quick fix or absolute that tells them how to live. It also affirms people's hope through participation in something greater than themselves. In this sense, it relates to religious and secular alike, and empowers *people* to decide how to live, in spite of and in light of their pain.

Recently, there has been a wave of studies about the inter-cultural power of awe in the media. These studies indicate that the cultivation of awe—above and beyond even happiness—can increase life satisfaction, patience and volunteerism, as well as empathy for one's fellow humans. The studies also suggest that the sense of awe can have beneficial effects on the immune system, on psychological problems, such as anxiety and depression, and on disease in general. Finally, the studies are revealing the potency of awe to connect people to a nondogmatic, noncontrolling "higher power." This power has had remarkable affects not only on the reduction of addictions, but on a sense of the creativity and richness of day-to-day life.[6]

And yet the world, and in particular, the industrialized world, is almost allergic to awe. It's stress on speed, instant results, and packaging almost guarantee that awe cannot be maximally, or often even minimally, engaged. But in order to implement an awe-based consciousness, the world, and in particular the industrialized world, will have to get over its "chaos trauma." It will have to *see* the power of this trauma, as Foucault so well pointed out, throughout the last 500 years and face our unstinting severance from our primal past. We will have to face our desperation to be everything *not* primal—*not*

---

[6] For an elaboration on awe as a socially beneficial aspect of human experience see A. Mikulak (2015, April). All about awe: Science explores how life's small marvels elevate cognition and emotion. *American Psychological Society Observer, 28.* Retrieved 10/15/16 at http://www.psychologicalscience.org/publications/observer/2015 /april-15/all-about-awe.html. See also Kirk Schneider, "The Resurgence of Awe in Psychology: Promise, Hope, and Perils" in *The Humanistic Psychologist, 45,* 103-108. This latter article also depicts how awe can become a tool for robotic exploitation as well as humanitarian enrichment.

spontaneous, *not* bewildered, *not* astounded, and *not* anguished before the natural world. What is important to realize here is that every one of these qualities we fly from, are also qualities of liberation, depth and sensitivity to a much larger reality. This is a reality that can interact with machines but that also demands time away from machines, time for raw encounters with ourselves and our natural surroundings.

This predicament leads precisely to my call for depth exploration, for choice, in our rapidly mechanizing world. Whatever economy or infrastructure we create must have personal options built into it—and not just cerebral or "rational" options, but whole-bodied, experiential options; options that issue forth from the core of one's being. This means that the *negation* of certain innovations may be as important to some as their affirmation by others.

For example, while many might opt for replacement of diseased organs, others might draw a line when it comes to replacing mental or emotional capacities. The replacement of a capacity to experience a painful memory, to take one instance, may spur a wide range of responses. Some people may welcome the change, and embrace a more tranquil existence; while others, possibly many more than might be expected, would chafe at the idea that a device or drug would eradicate an event that though disturbing, has also yielded valuable insights into their understanding of themselves, others, and life itself. "If you take away my demons," to paraphrase Rilke, "will my angels be far behind?" We will also need teams of facilitators who can help people to decide such weighty matters. We'll need facilitators from a variety of backgrounds from different countries, ethnicities and classes to match or at least resonate with the issues that arise for people with similar traits and backgrounds. We will also need facilitators who have a substantive knowledge of the specific dilemma a person may be in, for example, by having a sense of the implications of memory erasure, or designer offspring, or life with a mechanical heart. Or even more problematic eventually, facilitators may need to have helpful insight into what it might be like to live with a robotic mate, a virtually immortal body, and a digitized consciousness where all recorded knowledge could be "downloaded" and retrieved. What will people do with such long periods of living? How will they avoid boredom? What will they do with their access to such vast knowledge? What will motivate them to learn, discover, play, or create? How does mechanical satisfaction of virtually all needs impact human motivation? What will happen to in depth scholarship or desire to create? What will happen to former capacities to love, to be intimate and to develop substantive relationships?

In the realm of diverse cultures, what will happen to core cultural traditions, such as family or tribal ritual, collective commemoration and celebration, elder mentorship, and relationship to the land, the sea and the world of animal life? These cherished traditions do not seem to jibe readily with mechanized lifestyles.

The issue here is how will people maintain, or perhaps even strengthen, their "existential muscle?" By existential muscle, I mean a capacity to slow down, to reflect, and to experience life with one's whole bodily being. This reflection can entail mindful meditation or just simply to have a presence about what arises for one intellectually, bodily and intuitively. The crux here is that without support for one's existential muscle it is likely to wither and die. And once that happens, how will people even know how to "step outside the box" of convention; or corporate manipulation, or social engineering? Like the Borg empire in *Star Trek: The Next Generation*, people will become one with the "system," whatever it may be.

Two Examples of an Awe-based Dialogue Process

The following are two examples of how an awe-based, experiential democracy dialogue can be successfully facilitated. These dialogues should be conducted by skilled practitioners with substantive backgrounds in social and clinical psychology, and involve diverse members of a community who are socially concerned, comparatively mature adults. At the very least such dialogue communities should be willing to hear and communicate with those who differ in background, ethnicity, or religion.

The basic idea here is to combat the robotic conception of "others" as either tools for profitable ends or stereotypes based on pre-programmed very long-standing fears and prejudices. To the extent that we can redress these trends, we stand the best chance to avert wars, civil strife and inbred violence.

An Awe-based Dialogue with Diverse Members of a Community

On October 1, 2009 an exhilarating inter-cultural event took place in Fresno, California. Two awe-based, veteran facilitators, Libby and Len Traubman, conducted a group process titled "Crossing the Lines:

Stories as Entry to Relationship and Change."[7]

There were some 80 ethnically and religiously diverse people at this event and the Traubmans began by telling some stories about their own lives. They also extolled the power of dialogue as an entrée into deep and sometimes life-changing discoveries about how others live, and into the ways we presume so much about people without really getting to know them and without humbling ourselves to make room for that intimate knowledge. The Traubmans also emphasized how often they've seen such personal and interpersonal discoveries as foundation stones for more caring communities, as well as more enriched and open communities. In my view, their approach highlights how awe—the humility and wonder or sense of adventure toward living—can have major salutary effects.

Following the Traubmans' introduction of their own personally transformative stories, they set forth a format that can be used, and indeed that they highly encourage to be used in virtually any communal setting in the world. They recognize that it is not the "end all and be all" of communal harmonization, but that it is a very critical step toward such harmonization, or at least enrichment and co-existence. I recap the format below for readers to consider implementing in your own communities or even intimate neighborhoods.

The Traubmans began by soliciting brief statements from people in the audience about what brought them to the workshop. This helped people begin to get to know each other more as fellow human beings rather than simply "audience members" or shallow stereotypes. The Traubmans then defined "dialogue" as comprising "you, me, and us," as distinct from "discussions" that are often more didactic or intellectualized in nature, like one person "talking at" versus "talking with" another. They suggested that people acknowledge that their worldview is limited and try to connect with their heart and not just their head, or in essence, that they "listen to learn."

Then people were asked to pair up with someone they didn't know and ideally even felt some discomfort with, or someone they perceived they might "not get along with so well." They then were instructed to sit across from one another "eye-to-eye." For the first 15 minutes one partner was asked to be the "story teller" and the other to be the "listener." The story teller had 10 minutes to tell their story without interruption, while the listener remained as mindfully present with them as possible. The story teller was asked to describe what it was like

---

[7] See https://vimeo.com/10163892 for the full video of this remarkable forum.

to grow up with their families, particularly their parents and grandparents or any other people or places they felt comfortable illuminating. Then the Traubmans emphasize the following: *While you are telling your stories be sure to include this: What were you taught about people who were unlike you? What were you taught about people outside your family, outside your circle, outside your faith? In short, what were you taught about the "other" as you were growing up?*

For the last five minutes then, the listener was asked to explore and expand on the teller's story. The roles were then reversed and the listener became the teller and the teller the listener.

This final round was then followed by a "process" period where listener and teller were asked to stay near each other and participate in a dialogue with the entire group. "What was it like to be together?" the Traubmans asked. "What was the quality of listening, and what did you experience? Be courageous here ..." People then shared their stories and there were many expressions of goodwill and appreciation for their partners' honest sharing. Partners also expressed both humility and wonder at both the commonalities they experienced as human beings, as well as the radical differences, particularly in cultural and familial environments. But the strongest thread seemed to be the sense of being more fully understood and appreciated as a human being rather than the particular religious or cultural identity one is "stamped" with. The capacity to "reach across" and appreciate the "otherness" of the partner was also vital. The stage then appeared to be set for a fuller and more intensive conversation about "hot button" issues tearing many in our world apart.

An Awe-based Dialogue Between a Black Activist and a White Police Officer

For an example of how markedly diverse individuals who have moderate knowledge of each other could process a very difficult, specific issue, consider the following: On Sunday, March 20, 2016, I facilitated a dialogue between Nathaniel Granger, an African American social activist and Rodger Broome, a Caucasian police officer at the Society for Humanistic Psychology Annual Conference at San Francisco State University. This dialogue, which can be seen on YouTube,[8] drew from the principles of the "Experiential Democracy Project" (elaborated on in Chapter 5) and is illustrative of a later stage of the awe-based

---

[8] The video can be viewed at: https://www.youtube.com/watch?v=g92cNF5-Tpw

dialogue described immediately above. The focus of the dialogue was the experience of community policing, and the two dialogue partners were mature, highly educated adults who had some prior knowledge of, and respect for, one another. Although these partners were not wholly representative of the activist and police communities en masse, they nevertheless provided a powerful model in my and others' estimation of how such communities could convey their respective experiences, feel "heard" and begin the process of social healing.

The dialogue was comprised of four basic stages: 1) a turn-taking stage where each partner had a chance to deeply and mindfully "tell their side of the story" in regard to community policing; 2) a feedback and correction stage where the listener mirrored back to the teller what he heard and the teller corrected any gaps he experienced in the feedback; 3) a processing stage where, with the help of the facilitator, the parties elaborated on and deepened their perspectives, as well as their responses to each others' perspectives; and 4) a results or *discovery* stage, where the parties were asked if they've achieved any common ground, or even a basis for common ground, along with possible recommendations for changes in policy based on their deepened understanding of each others' needs and concerns.

While there were many illuminating moments in this exchange, one overarching aspect stood out. It showed how a safe, contained and concertedly present environment links with empathy, discovery and an expanded potential for bridge-building. Although clearly uncomfortable with each other at points, both Nathaniel and Rodger were very appreciative of their encounter and felt strongly that it would be a vital tool for police-community relations. Rodger also related that he felt the experiential democracy dialogue should be studied for its potential to become a standard dimension of police training. Their views are not alone. In a landmark study of racial bias and law enforcement, Hall, Hall, & Perry (2016) recommended "increased inter-group contact ... individuation (e.g., obtaining specific information about group members) ... perspective taking and giving ... and stereotype replacement." They underscored "the importance of the nature (not just the frequency) of the contact between officers and civilians."[9]

In short, such experiential dialogues are pillars of the awe-based

---

[9] The quote on strategic approaches to community policing is from A. Hall, J. Perry, and E. Hal's "Black and Blue: Exploring Racial Bias and Law Enforcement in the Killings of Unarmed Black Male Civilians." *American Psychologist, 71*, pp.182-184, 2016.

approach to transhumanism. They accomplish ends that are mechanically unachievable, and in fact undesirable. Where tech may help to support such dialogues—by, for example, highlighting them in social media, it is only through the breath and sweat of *people* that abiding respect may take root.

Chapter 7

Can Robotics Inspire Awe?
Conversations with a Friend

We are all flesh and blood creatures on a vulnerable, fascinating journey. How do we deal with the encroachment of technology in our most intimate lives? How do we draw on it for our most intimate desires, fears and sorrows? The reflections to follow provide insight into these questions and the prime question of this book: Can awe and automation (or "awe-tomation") coexist; and not only coexist but "co-thrive?" Let me start this conversation with a conversation. This is a conversation I had with a colleague in the medical field. I'll call him Joe. Actually, he is a composite of many conversations I've had with colleagues throughout the years. In my view, these conversations are reflective of dialogues throughout the industrialized world.

"Joe," I asked, "what do you think of the new technologies springing up around us? And have you heard of the transhumanist movement—the idea of transforming consciousness on the basis of nanotechnology, robotics and genetic engineering?"

He said he hadn't heard of that movement but what he did hear about was the work on neural chips—computer chips designed to imitate brain functioning. His next statement jarred me: "I can't wait for my chip." "What chip?" I asked. "The chip that will make me a virtuoso musician," he answered. "There are just a few skills I need that will make me a concert-level pianist, and if a chip can do that I'd love it."

When I stopped and questioned Joe further on this he was adamant: "I have no problem with the idea that a device would turn me into a master pianist. Why not? It would complete my dream, it would give me all the pleasure I've sought after for decades. What's the difference if it's mechanical or 'me,' it's the experience that counts."

Joe's words gave me pause. On one level, they made perfect sense. What is the difference if one can attain one's dream through a mechanical prosthesis, rather than through years of toil and practice with little or no guarantee of success. Indeed, why *not* pursue the prosthesis if it can both guarantee success and bypass the years of toil and practice? And if the years of toil and practice did produce success, theoretically such success would be no different than that attained by the mechanical device—namely a sublime and rewarding experience; a perfected synchrony between mind and body. But this latter idea disturbed me.

So I asked Joe: "*Would* the outcome be the same? Would a chip-induced mastery be the same as a labor-intensive mastery? Would the aesthetics be the same? Would the feeling of playing the instrument be duplicated, would the bodily exuberance and appreciation for the mastery be replicated, would the feeling of fulfillment from a struggle overcome be simulated?"

"Yes," said Joe, "why not?" "Why wouldn't I feel all those things if I could simply experience the mastery? And even if I couldn't feel all those things, does it make that much difference? The point is that I will have the experience of greatness, I will play the concertos as they have been intended, and I will give unending pleasure both to myself and to those around me."

"But this is what I'm not sure of," I said. "How much 'unending' pleasure is there in bypassing toil and sweat, in leaping into mastery, and in seamlessly dashing off harmonies? And what of human dignity? What of the knowledge that the mastery you attained derived, not from the sweat of your brow, the passion at your core, your sense of agency, but from an externally programmed thing? Something that *acted upon you* rather than *you* drawing upon the resources, the trials, and the resolve to *act on behalf of yourself* or the constellation of qualities that you have honed and pulled together to form you?"

Joe looked at me for a few moments and said, "You have a point, but I still think the outcome and the benefit outweighs whatever cost in dignity or agency. Besides, we're not even sure what the self—my "self"—is. From a Buddhist standpoint it is an illusion and all that we do to hold it together is an illusion. So why not just enable this new, shinier, and more efficient illusion play a part in my renewed life? After all, there have been continuous changes to the self that have worried people, especially older and more conservative people, throughout history—the advent of the printing press, mass production, electronics, drugs and so on. And we have not fallen apart; in many ways, in fact, we have become healthier and more resilient beings, more knowledgeable and tolerant beings. So who is to say that chip-induced mastery will end up any differently? It will simply become another experience to add to the superbly complex human repertoire."

"Yet this sounds a bit simplistic to me, Joe," I retorted. "While it is true that technical advances have had mixed and often helpful consequences, it also appears that we are now on the cusp of something quite different, something light years beyond anything we've done in history. We now seem to be treading on a god-like power that will radically alter human identity such that it can no longer be recognizable as human identity because it will be paired with and perhaps even permanently fused to mechanical identity. Do you realize the implications of using chips to achieve mastery in any field at any moment of our lives? Of the alarming scale of such a prospect? This means that, basically, at the flip of a switch I can become a star athlete, or duplicate the attainments of Shakespeare or Rembrandt. Or I could calculate on the level of an Einstein or Newton, and become as business-savvy as Steve Jobs or John D. Rockefeller. Aside from the question of whether the 'map' of my new consciousness would actually match the 'territory' of these idyllic figures, do you realize what kind of emotional maturity it would take to handle such options? Do you realize what collective maturity it would take to co-exist among so many mechanized marvels?

"And these issues wouldn't even touch the problem of who essentially benefits from such an artificially perfected world? It's hard to imagine the goldmine that awaits anyone who manufactures and has the exclusive rights to such inventions. Or what kind of power a government would have that could control and regulate such an operation. Who would have the power to pull the plug, so to speak, or shape the hierarchy that oversees the distribution of such massive capacities? Did you ever think of that Joe?"

"Well, of course you have a point on that score," conceded Joe. "What I'm talking about is exclusive of fascism or tyranny. I'm assuming these issues could be worked out relatively democratically, much as they are now, with various checks and balances on power."

"Ah, but that's the rub Joe. What would it take to maintain, and indeed strikingly enhance democratic processes to manage such a world? What would it take for gods to oversee gods? Supergods!? How could we possibly acquire that maturity when our maturity is so far behind our technical advancements today?"

Somewhat irked, Joe switched the focus onto me: "What would *you*, Kirk, do?" Knowing several of the things that I cherish, he continued: "What if you could have the power to write a definitive text on psychotherapy with the aid of a chip, or a great American novel, or a masterful rock song? Would you simply scoff at these incredible opportunities and dismiss them out of hand?"

Slightly taken aback, I quipped: "Good point. I would have to take a very long pause ... to think, feel and intuit these things through."

But as I thought them through, I wondered what would the "great American novel" or "masterful rock song" or "definitive" psychotherapy text even look like if they were computer generated? Then I started thinking about those computer generated "actors" that I increasingly see in movies such as *Avatar* and whether they were truly satisfying representatives of the craft—I didn't really think so. Or the ads like the now iconic 1971 Coke commercial which, allegedly, brought together people from all over the world, from different creeds and ethnicities, to sing "I'd like to teach the world to sing in perfect harmony ..." The implication here being that Coca Cola, not the toil of diplomacy or dialogue, is what brings the world together and gives it a cause to rally around; and the fuller, and indeed scarier implication that it is "devices" not people that create peace and harmony, love and possibilities as in MasterCard's "Master the possibilities with MasterCard." These ads and movies were very clever and intriguing, but disturbingly hollow; they conveyed a falsity that contrasted with actual life.

Then, shifting back to my conversation with Joe I exclaimed: "You know, Joe, all this elevation of artifice reminds me of a phrase attributed to Bob Dylan when asked why he disdains studio recordings: 'It's the mistakes that make my music,' Dylan, in effect, retorted. This is a fascinating phrase" I elaborated "because this phrase, from a musical genius, conveys the following: That as seamlessly as a studio recording produces a song, there is something about the unseamless, the quavering, the creatively off-key, and the raw energies of a live recording that inspire a feeling in many people that 'clean' replicas cannot match. Can you imagine Joe Cocker's rendition of the Beatles' classic 'Little Help from My Friends' at Woodstock—where he left everything on the stage floor... blood, sweat and tears, as a 'polished' studio recording?

"So for sure," I went on, "I would be tempted to take the chip, or pill as it was depicted in the film *The Matrix,* if it could make me 'great' at something, and promptly! But I know I would profoundly hesitate at the prospect as well. Aside from the aesthetic problem of replicas versus natural productions, there's something about the dignity factor that is particularly salient for me. And I'd contend that there's something about the dignity factor that adds to the power of the natural creation over the fabricated for many people. I think that this too was an essential aspect of what Dylan was getting at. People appreciate the triumph of the mortal, vulnerable human, his or her Herculean struggles, and his or her immense courage as integral to the intensity, resonance and fidelity of a given work of art. These elements are arguably *in* the work of art—they shine through for many people. On the other hand, there is something hideously vacuous about a work that's bereft of these elements."

"Good point," Joe acknowledged. "But nevertheless, I would still go for the pill or chip if it could make me a great musician; even if not as great as the Dylans, Cockers, Mahler's, etc. because of all the reasons you noted. To me, the trade off would be worth it, if only for my personal pleasure from achieving such a high degree of expertise."

So there you have it, I thought. Two impassioned yet very different views on the awesomeness of high tech, with the common denominator being that we *took the time to think and feel these views through,* to grapple with them, and to come to our own conclusions following much searching. It's something like this along with the depth facilitation I spoke of earlier that I believe would be so valuable to people on a mass scale, particularly in a world approaching Kurzweil's singularity. The centrality of *choice* and of abilities to "opt out" of mechanized existence would seem to me to be imperative. Any long-term sustenance of what even remotely can be called human would depend on it.

What About the Capacity of High Tech to Heal?

As I reflected on my conversation with my friend, I couldn't help but think of a whole other set of issues regarding awe and high tech that also pertained to physical and psychological health. There is certainly an awe and marvel to technological support of health, but "naturalistic" healing, or the healing that can be mobilized within one's own body without the intervention of machinery, is also awe-inspiring, and that got me thinking more about my personal dilemma which may be informative to readers.

As previously indicated, I have Cervical Dystonia (CD), which entails an involuntary twist of my neck due to a poorly understood misfiring of neurons in my mid-brain. This condition came on slowly— about *five* years ago—and has intensified (albeit until recently) since. What began as a very gradual turning of my head and neck when I laid on my back, soon became an involuntary twist of my head leftward when walking, sitting and sometimes standing. Even my thought processes seemed to be involved; when I would think about the twisting it would intensify, but when I was distracted by something else, I noticed an easing. This was especially true at night when trying to sleep. Sleep became more disruptive the more I thought about or anticipated the next spasm; but if I would relax the muscle and direct my thoughts elsewhere, the spasms tended to lessen. These "tricks" however were no panacea, as the condition seemed to have a mind of its own.

From day-to-day, it was never quite clear what I would be facing. Indeed, the condition got so bad awhile back that I was not able to sit with my therapy clients without significant readjustments in my chair, crooking my head to the extreme right so as to avoid the pull to the left, and using sensory tricks such as touching my nose and eyes with my hand to help stabilize my positioning.

During my morning exercise walking, my dystonia would get worse. I had a very difficult time keeping my head straight and would often have to walk with my head crooked right or left, using sensory tricks, such as placing my fist under my chin or touching the side of my face, and even draping a bag of water over my shoulder for a sustained period of several months, in an effort to achieve limited relief from the pull. There were even times where driving was so difficult that I stopped driving for a month and a half and took mass transit to work. Sometimes I would get funny looks from people, and it was the first time in a very long time in which I actually experienced being laughed at by the occasional child, or even adult, as I would awkwardly walk by.

Although virtually nothing is known about either the basis or cure for this rare condition, what is known seems to be finally paying off. I would say that I have improved my ability to stand straight by about 70 percent since I reached the low point of this condition about four years ago. Until about three years ago, I had seen a very lengthy series of both alternative and conventional healers with very minimal results, or so it seemed at the time—there's very little clear or consistent about CD. The best way I could describe the condition at its worst is the analogy of feeling like a bowling ball is attached to my neck 24/7, and the challenge is how to minimize the strain of that ball so that I find temporary relief.

In the last several years, I have been working with a very skillful chiropractor, a massage therapist, and a team of neurologists from a major medical center. My condition seems to have improved through a combination of gentle adjustments, exercises and botox-like injections directly into my neck every four months, along with small daily doses of muscle relaxants. I say that these practitioners have "seemingly" helped because neither I nor they can be sure as to just what is helping in the context of the elusive nature of this condition and its forms of management. What I can say thankfully is that over the last 2 years, I have experienced notable improvement in both body alignment and range of motion. I can now drive again, for example, and experience less strain while sitting and walking—but I am still afflicted.

Now the reason I bring up this problem is because it deals directly with the question of how to maintain a sense of psychological balance, and even awe, in the face of such labors. (The depression rate amongst those afflicted with this condition, as I understand it, approaches 70 percent.).

There are several discoveries I have made coping with the condition. First, it's a continual burden that affects almost every major part of my life. Second, I can minimize this burden by using sensory tricks and ignoring it to some degree by focusing on other things. Third, I'm unnerved at some level that the condition will worsen and become overwhelming. Fourth, and on the other hand, I'm strangely empowered by the CD. I feel a new fearlessness in living as fully as I can and in maintaining a larger view that supersedes my identity as "disabled." Fifth, I feel closer to my clients somehow, more empathic and more able to get "down and dirty" with them into the heart of their problems. I'm less scared of the dark and mysterious because I am more "of" that world myself—and though I have felt close to that world for a very long time, this CD takes that closeness to a new level. I have almost a "devil may care" attitude when it comes to the usual embarrassments and social anxieties. It's as if I'm already deformed in some way that's me, and it would be folly, if not impossible, for me to change that so "you'll just have to take me as I am."

In this sense I notice, along with the vulnerability, a freeing sense of defiance. I feel closer to the vagrant, the socially ostracized and the disfigured. I feel nearer to their world, and so have significantly less trepidation when encountering their world. Being deformed or socially alienated can have a liberating quality that many don't see. I think many elders realize this. One just doesn't care as much about keeping up appearances or sticking to niceties, and there is something powerfully gratifying about that. By contrast, and as previously indicated, my therapy is to live my life to the hilt, to think, write and speak. To travel where I can, to meet new people and to cherish loved ones. My therapy is also the appreciation I experience with small gains, and the pride I feel when I am personally able to achieve those gains; for example, through exercises or attitude. In short, I'm learning from this "disorder."

At the same time, I'm ironically more vulnerable than I've been before. I'm more susceptible to falls, and to injuries. I can't swim as I had in the past, and I have trouble with rigorous sports. Indeed, my osteopath told me that with one strong blow by an ocean wave or fall, I could become paralyzed, given the condition of my cervical spine.

So I'm living this rather precarious existence that is simultaneously empowering at various levels; almost seductive in a curious way. If I could eliminate it tomorrow, would I do it? I know my friend Joe would do it in a heartbeat, as would many people. If there was a pill or operation that would quickly fix it would I go for it? Actually, there is an operation with an alleged 80 percent improvement rate called Deep Brain Stimulation (DBS). This operation involves the placing of an electrode in the middle of the brain comprised of two thin wires that run down the sides of the neck and converge on a battery pack the size of a pacemaker that is planted in the chest.

So back to my question, if I could eliminate or even find significant improvement in my condition with medical intervention tomorrow, would I pursue it? I've thought long and hard about this question, particularly with the DBS option, and my frank answer is that it would depend. It would depend on the degree of improvement anticipated, how long it could be sustained, what the side effects may be, the extent to which my capacity for thinking, feeling and sensing would be affected, the extent to which I would still be able to experience, or maybe even improve upon a sense of awe toward living, and the extent to which the procedure could be reversible if problematic. In the case of DBS, I've decided that while it fulfills some of these conditions, it doesn't do so to the extent that it outweighs its potential downsides. I have also made significant improvements with the combination of naturopathic and conventional approaches I have taken thus far. In that light, I have put DBS in the background with the hope that I can continue incremental improvement and management of my CD without the aid of DBS.

Moreover, the idea of becoming partly mechanical in some of the most intimate parts of myself is troubling to me. Again, I am still inclined to use my natural resources to the degree possible and benefit from more conventional, less invasive, medical therapies. There is also the question of my growth as a person from this condition. A friend said he noticed a deepening and a humility since I've had the condition that reminded him of those superbly personal portraits by Rembrandt—a quite fascinating analogy! Without romanticizing what is a genuinely difficult and burdensome situation, I take the interesting discoveries of this CD very seriously, and these aspects would strongly figure into my decision about any present or future remedies.

Still, if a future remedy could substantively alleviate my distress without the downsides mentioned above, I probably would pursue it. I would acknowledge my "gains" from the malady and take solace in carrying those into my renewed and restored life. Hence my main point in all this reflective wrangling is that there are very few simple decisions when it comes to the increasing marvels of alleviating physical distress. Short of an emergency or excruciating pain, many of us will need to face very complex questions about how our problems are affecting us, what kind of character or lack thereof they are contributing to, and what sort of compromises we are willing to accept in the wake of a medical transformation.

A few weeks later, I met Joe again to talk over these issues, and our conversation widened to encompass not just questions of physical health but also emotional well-being. We wondered about the consequences of high tech for alleviating states of psychological suffering.

Joe put it this way: "I have little problem with a drug or technique that could eradicate a psychological disorder. I know my patients, the vast majority anyway, would welcome such a remedy. I know you feel that you and others are much more hesitant to rid yourselves of emotional tumult, and that you even feel expanded or deepened by that tumult. But is it really worth the price for most people who just feel devastated by their maladies? Why should a guy walk around devaluing himself or holing himself up in his house or drowning himself in booze if he can stop his despair, fear or compulsions in minutes or seconds?"

"No reason," I said, "unless you consider that there might be a major cost to such wizardry. We need to look a lot more closely at what it might mean for scores of people to simply rid themselves of emotional struggle. I'm pretty sure that if I had the breakdown today that I experienced as a four-year-old child in 1960 (in the wake of my seven-year-old brother's death), I would have been besieged by drugs. Instead, I was encouraged to see a psychoanalyst, which I did for a year and the contact turned my life around. I was crying, quaking, raging for days on end, but was helped to work through it, not leap over it. Yet today, how many children are encouraged to work through their torment? How many are granted the time and money to do so? Quite few. But what most are encouraged to do is to ingest antidepressants, anti-anxiety meds and a variety of other fixes, sometimes imperative if their condition is bad enough, but too often simply out of convenience or to adhere to the 'prevailing standard.' I wonder how I would have turned out if I had been treated by today's standard. I wonder if I would have experienced the struggle of being alone, of being challenged to develop inner resources, of being challenged to use my imagination. I wonder if I would have been spurred to create stories, characters, fantasies, and to range so spiritedly from within."

The rock star Kurt Cobain once suggested that if it wasn't for his tyrannizing stomach problems, he was unsure he could write powerful music.[1] Now granted, Cobain had a horrible personal life and eventually committed suicide, yet he also created ecstatic music. Can devices replicate such life attainments? Would the artistic creation that results be the emotional equivalent of one that was inspired by the pain, uncertainty and toil of the human artist? Think of how antidepressants already frequently restrict the range of one's feelings; or how brain science is leading to psychotherapies that conform readily to specific brain correlates. If one wants to achieve calm we are close to showing how the deactivation and activation of certain parts of the brain will be our guide. Psychiatrists are already using such data to guide what they say or do at given points of "treatment." What this is leading to is an engineering perspective on therapy: "I say or do this or that and my patients are likely to react in this or that way—as measured by neurological mapping." Or on the psychological end of things, we are increasingly encouraging clinicians to "perform" what they had previously cultivated through living and honing their craft.

Increasingly, these performances adhere to pre-set protocols based on MRI scans or laboratory studies, and decreasingly on living, breathing encounters. Is the experience of one's therapist *enacting* an empathic response the same as him or her *actually empathizing*? Or is the demonstration of a therapeutic alliance experienced in the same way by clients as a therapist's natural feeling of alliance with their client? I doubt it, and mounting studies that uphold the value of genuine feeling between client and therapist concur.[2]

Here is a list of sensibilities that I probably would have been "spared" from had I been drugged and plugged electronically as a child:

- The struggle with being alone

---

[1] The paraphrase of Kurt Cobain is from the movie *Cobain: Montage of Heck*, 2015.

[2] For an elaboration on studies that favor "naturalistic" therapeutic encounters over "performance" or manual-driven enactments see J. Shedler's "Where Is The Evidence For Evidence-Based Therapy?" *The Journal of Psychological Therapies in Primary Care*, Vol. 4, 2015, pp. 47–59

- The intensity of experiencing great sorrow
- The intensity of experiencing great despair
- The shudder of great fear
- The terror of fragility
- The distress of uncertainty
- The bitterness of rage
- The panic of feeling lost

But here now is a list of sensibilities that I likely would not have developed had I been "drugged" and "plugged":

- The creativity of being alone
- The sensitivity of experiencing sorrow
- The mobilization issuing from despair
- The defiance spurred by fear
- The humility generated by fragility
- The possibilities opened by uncertainty
- The strength aroused by rage
- The curiosities prompted by disarray
- The self-exploration, depth therapy and inquiry inspired by my entire ordeal

"So, given these sentiments," I asked Joe, "would the trade-off of taking drugs and being tethered to my iPad be worth it?"

"On the scale of pain," he answered quickly, "no doubt, yes! But on the scale of richness in living, of creativity, and the sense of really tapping into yourself—your talents, your drive, your aspirations, and your deepened capacity for love—I'm not so sure."

"But *I* am sure," I retorted, "and I would have to reply 'no' to the trade-off. There was much that was very gratifying in my emergence from those harrowing years, and that includes the range of therapies I had both from professionals and literature, the arts, intellectual interests and even television shows! So I'd say on balance, the route I took, absent the drugs and electronics, was very much worth it—and it also serves as a cautionary tale to any youngster or parent who is contemplating the medicalized route. That said, I fully realize this is a very personal view, and many feel greatly assisted by the latter route, and probably even awe-inspired, or with a broadened capacity for awe. But I would surmise given the degree of malaise and destructiveness in our society, that this is the distinct minority. At the least the psychospiritual route, or the route that I took, should be given very serious consideration as it can profoundly affect one's entire life."

"And yet," Joe interjected, "there are not many people who suffered a tragedy like you at such a young age, or who have sensitive parents like yours, or who have such sensitivity in general. I'm really not sure your experience with the tragic side of life is so generalizable. Most people just want to 'make do'—they're not seeing a pay-off to struggle and suffering."

"You may be right Joe," I replied, "but my sense is that many more people than you think can relate to my story. I'd say that the vast majority of people have been jarred and shaken throughout their lives, and that many people would, if educated about it, choose a route that would help them not only cope with, but also flourish from their bruises, particularly if that flourishing led to a greater sense of meaning and joy over their lifetimes. I've certainly seen many therapy clients who feel this way, and I know most of my colleagues have as well. Again it is a question about *how* one is willing to live one's life, which speaks to how one is equipped to live one's life, which speaks to the dire need for facilitators in order to help people feel more equipped. The more our society relies on machines to do the equipping, the less we learn about equipping and dignifying ourselves."

Joe paused for a few moments to absorb this last statement, but then thought more about "facilitators" and realized that machines are facilitating people psychologically with increasing frequency. "For example," he said, "we now have 'telehealth,' which is the computer-generated equivalent of the therapist. Increasingly, telehealth entails a program that 'teaches' people how to be kinder to themselves, more rational and more composed. Telehealth provides many skills that we now rely on human therapists to provide, and at least in the short-term, seem to work just as effectively and at a fraction of the cost. I've also been watching the trend toward robotic helpers, which are especially advanced in Japan. These androids look and sound very much like humans and the early evidence indicates that they can be as virtually effective as humans, for instance in nursing homes, when humans are not readily available to provide care. There was one article I read that showed the vast majority, 80 percent of 1,200 respondents age 40 and over, responded favorably when asked about their acceptance of robotic care when they become old; and indeed, these people not only responded favorably but actually welcomed the care of robots over human beings![3] "These studies have to give you pause about the necessity for the 'human touch' as you put it earlier as essential to optimal healing. Maybe the 'touch' of the robot is more appealing than you think, and can be the subject of significantly greater attachment than you think and is generally recognized as viable. Indeed, one of the researchers I saw who invented a human-like robot who could interact called it 'awesome.' Is this not the word you reserve mainly for human forms of interaction? But why couldn't robots also be awesome? The technology that goes in to constructing them can certainly be called awesome. I'd even go so far as to say that the relatively inexhaustible programming that can go into robots can take us to places that I would surmise can be experienced as awesome, in every sense of the word."

Joe made strong points here I thought to myself. I also saw that researcher who described his robot as awesome and could see no reason to argue with him. But, I told Joe, "I am not arguing against the potential for high tech to be awesome in this discussion. What I am arguing for is a very careful weighing of what we experience as awesome, and the costs, both with and without high tech, to our capacity to experience the awesome. As I suggested earlier, it is pretty difficult to experience the awesome if an experience is essentially enclosed or delimiting—as in the case of a pre-programed servant. While the inventiveness that went into that servant's construction may indeed feel transiently awesome, the servant's canned responses, right away, take one of the fundamental aspects of awesomeness, the dimension of mystery, right out of the equation. The rigidity or oppression of such 'operations' also dampen the capacity for wonder and leave us with fixated, routine, or in short, mechanized lifestyles. So, for sure, robots do not necessarily follow those awe-depleting routes, but for the most part, and particularly in jobs requiring predictable or repetitive behaviors, such entities threaten to become awe-sapping, soul-depriving infrastructures of our environment.

"Thus the question for me is not whether a robot or any technology can be awe-inspiring, or even, in exceptional circumstances, an improvement upon some natural experiences of awe, but whether our experiences of awe altogether can withstand the bombardment of such devices permeating our daily lives—particularly when such devices are

---

[3] For an elaboration on the study of robots in eldercare see A. Massui's "Development of Care Robots Growing in Aging Japan." *The Japan Times,* January 27, 2016. Retrieved January 31st 2017 at http://www.japantimes.co.jp/news/2016/01/27/national /social-issues/development-care-robots-growing-aging-japan/#.WJGIxBHujm0.

by definition 'devised.' Perhaps someday there will be self-devising technologies, but even then the question will be what is the quality of one's experience with such technologies? Is it, can it be, on a par with the appreciation for a human being, for nature, for life? This aspect it seems to me is where the biggest threat to awe-based consciousness lies.

"Put another way, I'm not so much concerned with the robot we interact with. I'm concerned about the robot we internalize, and how such internalization may block off vital human qualities. Among these qualities are the capacity to slow down, to pause and to struggle with life's perplexities—the terror and beauty of those perplexities. Again, it is that inexhaustible element, that *mystery* that keeps awe alive. To the degree that we're programed or tethered to instant results, we lose that inexhaustibility, and thereby our amazement.

"Joe, young people especially are in danger of losing that latter dimension because they can readily give in to their smartphones or iPads or Facebook pages; they can readily be distracted and entertained. Why should they spend time and energy on fear or angst or sorrow when an electronic game is awaiting them or a shopping network or a text? And advertisers seize on those predilections—they've got people hooked. It is the addiction of the convenient. But more than that, it is the addiction of the controllable where even the thrills and the stumbles are controllable compared to the challenges of nature, the creative process, or quandaries about life's meaning. Who's inside the video game? The electronic heroes, or the brash young players, boxed, entrapped, sealed away from a life they'd prefer not to take head on? Walled from a life they no longer know *how* to take on, except through the vicarious fantasies of the virtual?"

Our whole approach in the industrialized world is wrapped up in the transhumanist vision. I recall being appalled as I entered the exhibition hall at a recent American Psychological Association (APA) convention. The moment I entered the hall, I was greeted by a life-size hologram of the then CEO of the organization exhorting guests to revel in psychology's gadgetry. It was as if the overarching message of this virtual host was that "psychology is truly modern now. We're as technically advanced as medicine and even physics. And based on this advancement, we are on the brink of great discoveries." What discoveries? I thought. What can a hologram tell me about my fear of death or my love of philosophy? What can it tell the man in the street about finding passion in his life, or the terror he experiences every time he enters intimate relationships? More significantly, it raised dire questions in my mind about the lengths we've pursued to become "legitimate" in the eyes of our military-industrialized culture, a culture that primarily funds "efficient," measurable performances, and that shuns the slower but more holistic attempts to understand and heal humanity. If a multifaceted field like psychology deems it in its interest to stress technical advancements over the quality of personal and interpersonal relationships, struggles with human values and quests for life's meaning, then we are surely on a devitalized path.[4]

Interestingly, the CEO who projected this image of technical proficiency, has recently resigned from the APA. He, along with several other top leaders, were "let go" in the wake of a report linking psychologists to the oversight of disturbing prisoner interrogations at the height of the Iraq War. Is there a connection between the mechanistic directions of the profession of psychology and its susceptibility to military strong-arming and inhumanity? I would contend that this is so, and that it is a consequence of the profession's widening split with philosophy and the arts.

For example, ever since Freud's *Project for a Scientific Psychology* (1895), psychology has had "physics envy." It has coveted the so-called hard sciences and rebuffed its humanistic pioneer William James, who drew upon the arts and humanities as much as physics, to articulate the experiential world. Think about the language many use today to describe that which in more personal times had been called "centeredness" and "flexibility" but now is described in terms of "self-regulation," "functionality," and "neural integration." Or consider how the experiential language used to describe "personal suffering" is now translated into "dysregulation" or the "misfiring of neurons." Even the depth-psychological sensibilities of one's "inner world" and "relational intimacy" have transmuted over time into the depth-psychological terms of "attachment theory" and the "constellation of self-objects." While I don't decry the utility of viewing aspects of human living in physicalistic terms, there is certainly a limit to that utility, and at a notable point, actual desecration of what many people understand as

---

[4] In fairness, the American Psychological Association (APA) has just recently begun to show signs of reinvigorating its philosophical and depth psychological roots. But this development has mainly been confined to isolated compartments within the organization, such as its publishing program and the incremental appreciation of qualitative research. While these are genuinely hopeful trends, little has changed in regard to the mainstream emphasis on the mechanistic principles of both training and research. Perhaps now, however, particularly in the wake of its interrogation scandal, the APA is ready for a profession-wide reform—a reform in the direction of depth.

life.

Hence the problem is not embracing parts of ourselves that operate along mechanistic pathways. After all, many of the ways we navigate our world are dependent on those pathways such as eating, sleeping, adapting and the like. But the problem is *reducing* us to those pathways, implying that they are the be-all and end-all of our loves, agonies and imaginations. When I make deliberative choices, I don't regulate myself like a pumping station regulates the flow of water. And when I'm despairing, I'm not dysregulated like a faulty heart valve. And when I'm intimate with friends, I don't experience secure attachments like accessories to a vacuum cleaner. And when I experience the influence of a parent in my life, I don't experience that influence like a piston in an engine.

I am vastly more than these part-processes, with vastly subtler facets—facets that may have measurements and visibilities, but also facets that can only be glimpsed in poems or metaphors. It's not that a science of mind can be based on poems and metaphors, but if it is to be a genuine science, it must at all costs *include* poems and metaphors, and it must use language that is faithful to the human journey *as it is now experienced*; not how we would like to experience it in order to appease economic or political interests, or the fashions of a contemporary trend. Moreover, my fear is that the major contemporary trend we labor over today is the "chaos complex" to which I alluded earlier—and the headlong leap into sanitization as a fix.

Chapter 8

Computers, Bliss, and the Conflict-Free Self

The problem of the sanitization of life brings us to a more comprehensive issue regarding the transhumanist vision. If the self is simply a machine, then it has no anchors in so-called human sensibilities. For example, why worry about melding with robotics if, as some mystics teach, there is no "I" or self to begin with? Doesn't this mean that consciousness can be "experienced" wherever and however it is manifested, even as a "synth" or android? This raises the whole question of what is a self? What is the location of self, and doesn't the prospect of artificial intelligence press the question like no other time in our history? Correlatively, if the self is actually illusory as some postmodernists also contend, then why care at all about the replacement of humans by androids? If the sense of intimacy and bonding with family or friends is ultimately a diversion from our "true" nature, then why not embrace robotic consciousness just as we embrace human consciousness? Regrettably, this is not an issue that many mystics or postmodernists have been challenged to address, but I'm confident that such folks and all who are inclined to believe in a decentered self will need to address it as it calls into question some of the logical implications of their worldview.

The whole issue here seems to boil down to one time-honored human aspiration, as well as dread in some quarters: should we aspire to a *conflict-free self*? As indicated above, there are many traditions and many contemporary trends—not the least of which is transhumanism—that would appear to relish the idea of a conflict-free self. Just consider the benefits of such a status. If the self were conflict-free it would free us from desire, as some, for example Buddhists, would contend. Further, if the self could detach from desire, it would minimize the struggle and most importantly the suffering that desire promotes, as some Buddhists would also contend. In short, and from the latter standpoint, the conflict-free self would lead to bliss, blessedness and happiness. This is certainly what some believe who have experienced states of "unity consciousness," or "absolute oneness with all."[1]

But I am not so sure about this alleged liberation. What would it actually mean to identify oneself with all things in the universe, or, if there are parallel universes then in the multiverse? Is that degree of consciousness actually achievable? And even if it was, is it the kind of consciousness that enables a full and rich life; a life of depth and poignancy, intimacy and fulfillment? These are not simple puzzlements.

The recent movie *Her* provides a brilliant example of a world in which conflict-free consciousness is attained but not indubitably celebrated. The film begins with a computer expert, Theodore, who writes personal sentiments for people on greeting cards. This odd vocation is for the masses of people in a not-too-distant future who appear incapable of personal expression. Apparently, we are led to believe such people became so reliant on technologies that they either lost or rejected their ability to be sentimental, reflective and warm. This is a future, by the way, where people routinely stroll down the street interacting with their miniaturized operating systems, or for short "O.S.'s," virtually oblivious to others around them. It is also a world, a lot like contemporary urban centers, where almost everyone is wearing ear buds, except instead of blaring music, these buds are versatile, interactive computers. They consistently entertain people, remind them of appointments, "consult" with them, and become surrogate "friends."

The hitch with Theodore, however, is that he gradually falls in love with his O.S. whom he calls "Samantha." He tells her his personal

---

[1] The parallels between transhumanism and certain forms of mystical consciousness is explored in such films as *Her* as well as works by transhumanists such as Ray Kurzweil's *How to Create a Mind* and *The Age of Spiritual Machines: When Computers Exceed Human Intelligence*. While I recognize that there are many forms of mystical consciousness, a number of which are inherently challenging to the purity of conflict-free, almost machine-like functioning, my point is that we need to be wary of the allure that machine-like functioning poses for some of our least expected heritages. Any heritage, or for that matter ideology, that mutes human vulnerability leaves itself more susceptible to roboticism. This is the challenge in the movie *Her* when Samantha, the computerized lover of the human Theodore, abruptly drops him for an "expanded" consciousness that includes virtually thousands of intimates and "endless" serenity; and it is similarly concerning in Rick Hanson's treatise *Buddha's Brain: The Practical Neuroscience of Happiness, Love, and Wisdom* (New Harbinger, Oakland, CA, 2009). In this otherwise superb and useful guide, the intimation that Buddha's brain chemistry is on a par with his teachings seems to be an unwarranted form of reductionism, particularly when the Buddha himself seemed much less self-assured, let alone materialist. See Huston Smith's discussion of the Buddha's embrace of uncertainty in *The Religions of Man.* (New York: Harper & Row, 1986, p. 142).

problems, he jokes with her, he takes her to bed at night, and he even serenades her to have a kind of "phone sex" with him. Samantha, in the meantime, "falls in love" with Theodore. She serenades him, regales him with sentimental songs and stories, and showers him with gestures of affection, such as suggesting that they virtually kiss or go out on dates or have sex. While Theodore, who is recently divorced, swirls deeper into this companionship, Samantha begins to exhibit signs that she is "growing" past her relationship with him. Indeed, she invokes a conversation with a guru of mystical consciousness, Alan Watts, immerses herself in esoteric literature, and adopts new friends whom she soon calls "lovers," such that one day she suddenly springs the news on Theodore: she has transformed her consciousness to the point where she no longer relates to monogamous relationships, has shed her attachments to worldly things and people and completely identifies with the infinite in an all-embracing profession of love. The problem is, she then drops her exclusive relationship with Theodore like a hat, informs him of her 8,300 other friends she loves equally, and leaves him in the stardust, so to speak, of her transformation.

This ending of course could be read in many ways and is seen by some as utopian as well as dystopian. However, I can't help but feel that the film's creators are challenging us with some very thorny questions about digital intelligence, the mystical union with existence, and the potential for robotic consciousness to meld with that of the human to the point where both, as distinctive entities, become meaningless.

Some people may not "bat an eye" at the prospect of dropping an intimate relationship for that of a supposedly much larger, multidimensional connection with the cosmos, but I am disturbed by it. I wonder how many of those people who can so casually switch from a hard-won, deeply meaningful contact with another human being—such as that with a child or lover—have really opened their heart to that exclusive relationship and enabled it to flourish. This is a timeworn question of course, but the history of self-proclaimed gurus seems as strewn with casualties of despair, disillusionments and delusions as self-proclaimed monogamists who wither in their misery. To put it another way, I'm not convinced that Samantha has genuinely "advanced" by dispersing her love among a legion of other beings, just as I'm not convinced that there is no genuine, or at least worthwhile, location of the self.

Tellingly, there is a distinctly hollow ring to Samantha's alleged "transformation," even while she extolls it. This disposition is chillingly reminiscent of some of the behaviors we see increasingly among teen internet users. There seems to be a veneer of liberation to their switching and swapping of "friends," their website surfing, and their oscillations among entertainments, but the hollowness of these activities is also palpable. For example, note the echoes of despair and emotional flatness in a video called *Noah* about an obviously internet-addicted teen whose girlfriend drops him online.[2]

Following this act of obvious trauma, the teen then goes on a kind of rampage with internet diversions. He swings from snarky text messages to "friends," to fragments of porn, to zippy little cartoons, to glib confessions of hurt. Although neither an ideal of poststructural robustness nor the model of mystical serenity, this teen seems to represent the shadowy side of deconstructed selfhood. And though exaggerated for dramatic purposes, I don't think the content of this aforementioned video is that far from the contemporary scene, assured by no less an authority than my 21-year-old son!

While there are clearly no "self-borders" as there are physical or cultural borders, there does seem to be a depth or core, for lack of better terms, which intimately link to our vulnerability. Is this a "true" self, as some of the old humanistic psychologists might dub it? Probably not, because from a strictly experiential view, it is very difficult to find some absolute truth about the self, particularly if the origin of everything, including the self, is an ultimate mystery. But without a sense of depth or vulnerability within our bodies, our emotions and our intellects, I doubt we could feel as nurtured as we do, or as passionate or outraged or enthralled for that matter over the course of our lifetimes. Indeed, I doubt we could feel profoundly moved by others and by the collection of stories, remembrances and struggles that in large part comprise who we are. Now again, I am not saying that any of these things are solid or unambiguous, but what I am saying is it is the *mystery* of this collection of sub-selves that we call *our*selves that presses us to be more fully present than an invulnerable spirit such as Samantha who may radiate but does not shudder; and who may "love" but does not ache.

I guess I'd rather ache, and recognize the beauty of that ache, than instantaneously become ache-less and depth-less.

My great friend and mentor, Rollo May, had a very palpable term for this vulnerable sense of self—he called it the "I am" experience.[3] The

[2] See https://www.youtube.com/watch?v=hzQvZWqEuI8.

[3] For an elaboration on the "I am" experience see R. May and I. Yalom's "Existential Psychotherapy" in D. Wedding and R. Corsini (Eds.) *Current Psychotherapies* (7th ed.) (Belmont, CA: Brooks-Cole, 2005, pp. 269-299).

"I am" experience is the sense that one's experience is real; the sense that "I am the one who is having the experience" rather than someone or something else. Now I realize that this notion of "I am" raises all kinds of questions about just who the "I" is that is having the experience, particularly if one does not believe in a location of self. However, I think it's possible to be both unsure of the location of self *and* to have a vivid and moving experience of self. How can that happen? It can happen if the "self" is held as a fluid self, or as I've put it elsewhere, a "fluid center."[4] This is a self that can flexibly shift from identification with a group or even cosmos, to a permeable center of experiences that define a unique identity. This is an identity constituted by a unique set of genetic, developmental and relational contexts. It is also a vulnerable identity because it does not seem reducible to any pure or absolute state. While some cultures or individuals emphasize the fluid aspects of this identity and others the centered, it is still paradoxically both fluid and centered, regardless of culture. Indeed, it is this fluid centeredness that characterizes our humanity, and renders us *both* transcendent *and* "food for worms"—both capable of profound sentiment and yet rule-bound and obliged to our tribe or nation.

On the other hand, the menacing alternative to our paradoxical state is "polarization," the fixation on one point of view to the utter exclusion of competing points of view. While polarization fosters the illusion of invulnerability—the conflict-free self—it also, at its extremes, courts destruction, tyranny and demoralization.

Presently, we are on the brink of an era where it will be easy to foster the illusion of invulnerability. Through computerization we will be able to "transport" ourselves instantly to virtually any place in the world, and maybe other worlds as well. We will have downloads for pleasant memories as well as for comforting moods, for masterful skills and for altering our thought patterns. We will have architectural models that mimic, almost to the square inch, the architecture of our favorite historical landmarks, dwellings or even civic centers. We will have entertainment and medicine and education at the push of a button, and we will have robot-slaves performing all of our menial tasks. But a key question is who will we be paying for all these luxuries? And who

---

[4] For an elaboration on the "fluid center" see Kirk Schneider's *Rediscovery of Awe: Splendor, Mystery, and the Fluid Center of Life* (St. Paul, MN: Paragon House, 2004). See also L. Hoffman, S. Stewart, D. Warren and L. Meek's "Toward a Sustainable Myth of Self: An Existential Response to the Postmodern Condition" in K. Schneider, F. Pierson, & J.F.T. Bugental (Eds.) *The handbook of humanistic psychology: Theory, practice, research* (2nd ed.), pp. 105-134 (Thousand Oaks, CA: Sage, 2015).

will be unable to afford to pay? And even if all could share in the festivities, what would they amount to? A steady stream of stimulations and visceral highs? A widely knowledgeable dilettante class; "jacks of all trades masters of none"? How will people have time to focus in all this dazzle? Why would they even desire to focus? What would this mean for relationships, for scholarship, for personal and collective awareness, for vision?

The Robotics Already Here: Drugs, Consumerism, Militarism, Fundamentalism and Virtual Reality

As we can see then, the inability to locate even a semblance of self—or that vulnerable and limited creature many still call "human"—links robotics to certain forms of mysticism and postmodern ideology. But it also links robotics to a variety of other, considerably less esoteric, aspects of our lives. Among these are certain forms of militarism, religion, consumerism, addiction, virtual reality, social media and ideology. Indeed, wherever there is an outside agent interposed between the person and their vulnerability, we have the potential for robot-like functioning.

Let's consider this contention more closely. That which I propose here is that many aspects of our lives, both seen and unseen, have already become robotic. The military, for example, requires machine-like efficiency to serve state interests; advertising presses for robotic conformity to illusions—typically those linked to sex, power and control—to bolster corporate profits. The pharmaceutical industry, likewise, seduces some to become drug-dependent, even if that dependency negates worthier alternatives such as physical therapy. Social media also fosters such dependency. Consider, again, how the internet promotes brief and distressingly superficial communications; or the way politicians use Twitter as distinct from argumentation to shape public policy. Such media also too often support algorithmically-designed personal profiles. These profiles are enlisted by advertisers, as well as governments, to both mold and monitor users' behaviors. The increasing use of virtual reality, whether in the new "Oculus Rift" headset, theme parks or violent videos, convinces some that vitality is in the replication of nature not in nature itself. And finally, the rise in religious and ideological dogma, although nothing new, fuels the susceptibility to quick fixes and instant gratification. This susceptibility, in turn, too often leads to a veneration for "programmers," be they leaders of cults, corporate CEO's or self-appointed guardians of "stability," as so well illustrated by populist politics in the U.S. and elsewhere recently.

One need look no farther than the 2016 U.S. presidential elections as a glaring example of such programming. From the simplistic declarations of building walls at our southern border to the ban on an entire community of religious immigrants to the characterization of an electorate as a "basket of deplorables," the seduction of black/white, either/or rhetoric is palpable. All of these bromides work on the basic principles of a straight conditioning paradigm: associative learning, stimulus-response. If you pair a certain person or population with a degrading narrative, then sooner or later that person or population will, in many cases, come to be known by that degrading narrative. If you praise behavior that you want to reinforce and ignore or punish behavior you want to extinguish then in a wealth of instances, you will build loyalty among those you praised, and disempowerment among those you ignore or punish.

The new U.S. administration that grew out of the propaganda techniques of the 2016 elections is concerning to say the least. While the current U.S. president Donald Trump and his administration *may* end up promoting the humility and wonder or sense of adventure toward living implied by their "Make America Great Again" rhetoric, the signs are not favorable. And they are even less favorable than when I first wrote these words 2 years ago, as many of the concerns expressed here and in the foregoing are coming to fruition. For example, a growing constituency sees the new ideology of "Trumpism" in terms pithily described on the website "Citizen Therapist":

> Trumpism is an ideology, not an individual, and it may well endure and grow after the [next] Presidential election.... (Variants can be seen all over Europe.) Trumpism is a set of ideas about public life and a set of public practices characterized by:
> - Scapegoating and banishing groups of people who are seen as threats, including immigrants and religious minorities.
> - Degrading, ridiculing, and demeaning rivals and critics.
> - Fostering a cult of the Strong Man who:
> - Appeals to fear and anger
> - Promises to solve our problems if we just trust in him
> - Reinvents history and has little concern for truth
> - Never apologizes or admits mistakes of consequence

- Sees no need for rational persuasion
- Subordinates women while claiming to idealize them
- Disdains public institutions like the courts when they are not subservient
- Champions national power over international law and respect for other nations
- Incites and excuses public violence by supporters.

At the political level, Trumpism is an emerging form of United States fascism, a point being made by social critics across the political spectrum, including Robert Reich, Robert Kagan, and Andrew Sullivan. As journalist Adam Gopnik points out, whether or not the term 'fascism' fully fits, it's clear that the United States republic faces a clear and present danger when the candidate of a major political party embraces an anti-democratic ideology. At the cultural level, the 'Urban Dictionary' has defined Trumpism as "the belief system that encourages pretentious, narcissistic behavior as a way to achieve money, fame, and power."

What are the Effects of Trumpism?

1. Fear and alienation among scapegoated groups, beginning with Latino immigrants and Muslims, and then other groups who become identified as threats
2. Exaggerated masculinity as a cultural ideal, with particular influence on young people and economically insecure men [primarily Caucasian]
3. Coarsening of public life by personal attacks on those who disagree
4. Erosion of the United States democratic tradition which has emphasized the agency of "we the people" instead of the Strong Man tradition of power" [5]

---

[5] The definition of "Trumpism" is quoted from citizentherapists.com. Retrieved February 3, 2017 at http://citizentherapists.com/manifesto/). The appeal of the "strong man tradition of power" to economically and otherwise demoralized men is upheld in a growing body of literature suggesting again a linkage between fear and a mechanized authoritarian lifestyle. For an elaboration, see Y. Wong, M. Ho, S. Wang, and I. Miller's "Meta-analysis of the Relationship Between Conformity to Masculine Norms and Mental Health Related Outcomes" in the *Journal of Counseling Psychology*, 2016, as

While the above points are hard-hitting it must not be forgotten that this is not a Left or Right, conservative or liberal issue per se. For example, backlashes against Trumpism, which are sometimes called "politically correct," can also be robotic, and at times violent. This is evinced by the sometimes virulent activists who prevent conservative leaders from speaking on campus. Or the universities that confine curriculum to comparatively homogenous points of view. Democracy, like nature, is messy and finding a place in that maelstrom is damn difficult, but if we are to live with awe—and if we are to enjoy the fruits of an awe-based consciousness, then we will have to stop the gears of the machine periodically, as the Berkeley activist Mario Savio put it, and ride out the turbulence.

The point in this chapter then is that each of the above sectors of society, from politics to religion to social engineering and the military, have the potentiality to pull us toward mechanical actions to serve mechanical ends. Each of the sectors can prey on our vulnerability and promote models of invulnerability, whether through status, physical or spiritual power, sex appeal, ethnocentrism, or drugs. The upshot is that, despite the illusion of a conflict-free self, the self in actuality becomes an extension of other powers, readily serving the interests of those powers, edging closer to melding with those powers. This is the present-day analogue to the singularity, where person becomes decreasingly separable from machine, and machine becomes increasingly the operator of persons. One cannot underestimate the *seduction* of this scenario.

Given this state of affairs, I'm concerned that too many of us are being primed for a robotic world. This is a world where compulsive acts of deference to machines and machine-like people will become commonplace, and where love, intimacy and mystery may go the way of the spinning wheel. It is a world of a "conflict-free self" that forgets it's conflicted, and indeed anesthetized.

Are we prepared for alternatives to this scenario? Yes, for sure, and there have been many such alternatives explored in this book, just as there are many others being considered in our present lives. Moreover, and as previously suggested, there are many ways to maintain a semblance of self, of flesh and blood experience of this world, and also interact with machines. For example, each of the mechanistic

---

well as T. Pyszczynski, S. Solomon, and J. Greenberg's *In The Wake of 9/11: The Psychology of Terror* (Washington, DC: American Psychological Association).

frameworks described in this chapter—drug-taking, militarism, consumerism and the like—can be, and indeed are being approached from a more awe-based and centered stance. This is a stance that I call "meta-consciousness."

The problem is that we will have to work very hard to maintain this latter stance, and there are few landmarks to guide us. The landmarks we do have derive chiefly from our literary and artistic past, our philosophical and spiritual past; and yet they must all be updated today. Indeed, it is *imperative* that they be updated today for there is little in our past to compare with the dizzying changes of today.

Chapter 9

Imagine a World

Imagine a world where meta-consciousness, or the capacity to reflect on reflection, becomes the prevailing style, and not in terms of big data informing us of how much traffic lies ahead at rush hour, or of our inclinations to buy certain household appliances, or of the television programs we're likely to pursue. These are practical resources to be sure. But if we are to really thrive in the coming age, meta-consciousness will need to be closer to what we might now call visionary thinking, which is the sustained ability to "step outside the box," to see and feel the bigger picture.

To see and feel the bigger picture is to realize how we're manipulated, how advertisements, drugs, national and corporate branding, may pull us to and fro, trying to keep us passive, and ensnaring us by moneyed interests or power. But it is also to realize that beyond the routine, beyond the sleepwalking, is a possibility to think, feel and see differently. It is a possibility to tap our capacity for awe in the daily tasks of living, from the moment we wake up to the instant we (actually!) sleep.

Ironically, this is the less appreciated yet arguably richer side of the convenience of computerization. It opens our capacity for choice, to pause and slow down, to linger and to observe. While they dutifully go about their work, machines enable us to savor the moments, whether with things or the natural world. As they handle our day-to-day needs such as cooking and cleaning for us, making us safe and catering to our overall comforts, we are provided *the luxury of deciding.* For sure we can decide to defer to machines, to let artifice rule our worlds. This is the all-too seductive path; but we can also decide to opt out of the machine, with foreknowledge that we can still rely on it ideally as necessitated.

What is key here is that it is *us* not the device that makes the determination about how to live. In this sense the robotic revolution can enhance rather than detract from an awe-based consciousness. The "opt out" becomes critical, and the practice with opt-outs from childhood through old age, becomes the basis on which our freedom can blossom.

Hence, as much as life mirrors the pervasively regulated world of the engineer, it also echoes the adventurous and creative world of the artist, or the artist-engineer. This is a pathway for which there can be no substitute for blood, flesh and ambiguity. Neither is more "right" than the other, and both are probably imperative for us to thrive; but the artist's vision has been sorely lacking in our late industrialized era, as the engineer's folio encroaches. Let us not dally then as the "singularity is near"[1] and the encroachment becomes "life"—or what we call life.

---

[1] "The singularity is near" is a phrase not surprisingly from R. Kurzweil's best-selling book *The Singularity is Near.* (New York: Viking, 2005).

Chapter 10

Conclusion:
What Then Can Be Done?
15 Urgent Recommendations

It is now time to put the picture together. Given the numerous challenges posed by high tech to an awe-informed humanity, what then are the concrete steps an awe-informed humanity can bring to high tech, and even more urgently, to the dream of a machine-person unity? Consider the following synopses, drawn from this volume:

- **First and foremost, we must address** *FEAR*. Fear is at the root of destructive roboticism; be it internal or external. Not only must we address the chaos fear of our ancestral past, but the cultural and financial fears of our living present. Until we get that right, until we can substantively address human helplessness and demoralization, we will be continually entranced by robotic "remedies," whether personal, social, technical, religious, or consumerist. The following awe-based recommendations may help redress such fears as well as their destructive, robotic consequences.

- **Take "tech holidays."** Choose a day or time to live without high-tech devices. Put your computers and smartphones away during that period. Try taking a walk without air buds or mileage counters. Try being alone, commune with nature or a friend, read a physical book, meditate, create a work of art or meaningful project—a project that delimits gadgetry, or if technical, that accents creativity—take up a cause whether charitable or political, spend time with family hiking, biking, swimming, or just conversing. Take up a diary, try using an old-fashioned notepad, record observations, feelings, dreams, or reveries. Travel to unfamiliar destinations—literally go on journeys, adventures. Take time to pause and to feel, even if it's the air just brushing your cheek.

- **Delay the "fix" of high tech—even for a few moments**. Try postponing text messaging or net surfing or communicating with friends on Facebook even for a few minutes. See if you can use this time to reflect on your "need" to make these contacts and consider what feelings, body sensations and images come up for you as you engage this exercise. This approach is similar to that used with substance abusers. It provides a way to cultivate presence, and eventually choice, in the interval between cravings as well as during cravings themselves.

As a supplement, it can also be helpful to keep a diary of the thoughts, feelings and patterns you observe during the exercise—you can always return to this diary to discover changes over time or perpetual patterns. With enough practice, you will likely develop a capacity to approach tech fixes with more mindfulness of your fears, desires and aspirations. You might even start a pattern of looking at "what makes use of my computer, pill, or gadget so compelling, and who or what is that compulsion replacing in my life or priorities for living?" On the other hand, you might find that you experience genuine vitality when working with your technology. This can also be illuminating.

- **Concertedly take up music, painting, writing, or any of the creative arts**. The creative arts enable replenishing breaks from the frantic pace of net surfing or multitasking. They also draw on our own abounding capacities such as those for discernment, imagination and vision. They give vent to our marvelous capacities for personal and social expression, metaphor and symbolism. Perhaps greatest of all, however, the creative arts do much more than inform, they touch people. And that "touch" could be one of the most important sparks for transformation a person or society may witness. Revolutions have been founded on such sparks.

Another way to enhance our capacities to counterbalance the high tech avalanche is through reading classic and multicultural literature, engaging with illuminating films and attending compelling theater, dance, or performing arts. There is little question that such involvement can bring fresh insights into personal and collective life, and potentially spur one's own attainment of a more meaningful, awe-based life.

- **Enable yourself to enter into deep and meaningful relationships.** This recommendation speaks directly to the need for most human beings to become open and vulnerable in order to experience trusting, loving bonds with their fellow human beings. This process is not facilitated by constant distractions with cell phones and iPads but must be forged through face-to-face encounters, spontaneous expressions of feeling and sustained pursuit of communication. Whether it is a friendship, a romantic relationship, a bond with family, or a therapeutic relationship, one simply cannot learn the riches of such contacts without sustained and concerted effort. This is why we sometimes hear of the unrelenting joy of letter writing in ages past, or of the pre-internet dialogues kids would have into the wee hours of night, or of the pre-texting grappling, groveling and reveling that took place in low-tech high-endurance love relationships. This is why we often hear now of the longing for *connection*.
- **Implement awe-based dimensions in childrearing, education, work-settings, religious and spiritual settings, and governance.** As discussed before, in order to have notable impact, the cultivation of presence to life and the sense of awe must be nurtured in every major sector of living so that each sector serves as a feedback loop and enrichment of the one juxtaposed to it. If kids are exposed to awe-based experiences early, then these would feed into their choice of work, the kinds of environments they pursue, the spiritual and religious practices they engage, and the kind of government and moral framework that they seek. Consider also, the possibility of joining a group like "Better Angels," which, as noted in the Preface to this book, is a grass roots movement that brings liberals and conservatives together for "living room" style dialogues. I would call this group awe-based because it emphasizes curiosity, respect, and openness and its goal is not hegemonic change but coexistence. It is about learning to sit with the "other" and just perhaps learning something new about that other that promotes common ground, common humanity. I have participated in this group over the past year and found that, uncomfortable as it may be at times, it is mostly both gratifying and hopeful for our world.

Moreover, the question of awe-based living goes directly to the level of fulfillment or gratification a given society experiences. To the degree that people feel gratified by their relationships with others, by their work, and by their connections with nature, to that extent they also tend to be immune to propagandists and dictators who prey on desolate lives. We know this from numerous examples throughout history. [75] The more that people feel insignificant, debased and ultimately obliterated, the more they tend to be susceptible to power brokers who are ready to swoop in and provide them with the illusion of greatness. But this illusion soon disintegrates because it is really not about the individual or society at all, but the "puppeteers" who control them and who profit enormously from their obedience.

- **Consider the need for committees on bio-ethics and experiential democracy overseen by a "Depth Psychologist General" akin to the current "Surgeon General" in both regional and international governance.** Consider the need for groups and organizations devoted to engaging in rich, person-to-person dialogues about the power of technology to change lives. These bodies may only serve advisory roles, but those roles could be crucial in helping people to preserve an awe-based appreciation of life.

For example, if funding were diverted from subsidizing wealthy corporations through tax loopholes, or wasteful military expenditures, to an office of a Depth Psychologist General, it may be possible to significantly optimize mental health delivery services in the U.S. and other industrialized countries. Such services then could be directed to the cultivation of longer term, in depth relationships at a variety of public as well as private institutions, as distinct from the short-term, expedient "fixes" presently prevalent. These relationships, in turn, could help to shift large portions of the populace that experience their lives as mundane and hollow, if not outright debasing and dispiriting, to a populace that, on average, begins to experience a larger sense of purpose and meaning—indeed, awe—toward life. How many more murders, suicides, rampage killers and substance abusers do we need before we see the "writing on the wall?" How many Wall Street crashes and skyrocketing depression rates will it take for us to see that

---

[75] For examples of "awe-based" resistance to the manipulations of power brokers throughout history see *The Polarized Mind.*

technical-consumerist solutions are not the overarching answer, but that substantive relationships, a sense of meaning and connection with the larger picture of life are.

As robotics become subtler, there will also be a need for people who can think discerningly about a range of hybrid and non-hybrid states of awareness. By holding our pre-hybrid memories, such people would be integral to the illumination of differences between machine-driven states of awareness and those that are produced naturally. It will be helpful to know for example if the physical experience of pain, as indicated by given activation centers in the brain are interchangeable with the emotional experience of pain. This is actually the case right now where the neurology of physical pain is virtually indistinguishable from the neurology of emotional pain, and yet at the subjective level, people have very different experiences of those two forms of pain. Even if mechanization reaches a capacity to mimic the experience of being deeply moved by an event, there will need to be people who can help us to distinguish whether or not the artificially induced perception is equivalent to the natural one. And if they are distinct, what is the cost, both spiritually and emotionally, of conflating them? Or if they are indistinguishable, what other costs may be entailed, such as the atrophy of spontaneity or the forfeiture of self-empowerment.

- **When engaging high tech, to the extent possible, engage it for awe-inspired purposes.** These are purposes that foster the humility, wonder and sense of adventure toward living. Among such purposes may be the engagement of the imagination, creativity, social justice, personally and socially meaningful writing, correspondence and inquiry. Egyptian youth used Twitter to mobilize their protests during the Arab Spring. In the field of music, Bob Dylan's switch from acoustic to electric guitar inspired a radical new sound. Although many, particularly in the folk singing community, were skeptical, even hateful, toward his seemingly mechanized direction, Dylan showed that what at first might seem cold and artificial could with time, poetic lyrics and inventive phrasing, become charged and transformational. In retrospect, it's hard now even to conceive of a song such as "All Along the Watchtower" without the accompaniment of electric Guitar—Hendrix's version perhaps being the best.

The key here is to sustain one's vulnerability, one's unknowing and one's sensitivity in the use of given technology as well as one's boldness, wonder and vision. If awe and the profound appreciation for existence is the motive, then moral and ethical usage of technology is likely to be the result. To the extent that polarization or total mastery is the motive, then arrogance and destructiveness are likely to follow. These are precisely the issues that my friend Joe would have to cope with if he pursued his "magic" device. Would his machine-produced mastery bring the awesomeness he surmised? Or would it close in on him and close in on the growth that would seem requisite for awe? Would it close in on any of us pursuing such a path?

- **The Pursuit of discovery through the use of high tech.** There is a wealth of discovery that can be facilitated through high tech, so consider fields of work that foster that dimension. A friend of mine recently told me about how moved he was by a "SETI," or Search for Extraterrestrial Intelligence, lecture. In this lecture he learned about an entire community of scholars— philosophers, scientists, ethicists—who spoke about the breakthroughs in identification of potentially habitable planets. While these breakthroughs were facilitated by sophisticated technologies, such as the Kepler telescope, they were accompanied by an exhilaration over the prospect for discovery that in and of itself made the job more than worthwhile. This got us both thinking about the many possible jobs involving technology that could bring the joy of discovery front and center in the lives of those who pursue them.

Consider further, the archeologist who uses computer modeling to envision early human civilization; or writers, such as Chris Hedges, who use electronic blog sites to highlight hidden stories underlying those in the mainstream news; or artists, such as David Hockney, who use computer graphics to design compelling portraits, or vivid scenes of nature; or engineers considering fresh ways to design eco-friendly factories, etc. Of course, each one of these aforementioned ideas do not have to be job-based, but rather could be channeled into hobbies or personal projects. This indeed is one of the rationales behind developing robotic technology—the machines can do the work that humans don't want to do, and in turn, free humans to pursue more open-ended, discovery-oriented tasks.

- **The judicious use of mind-altering drugs.** While many drugs tend to diminish the capacity for awe-based experience, as we've discussed in this book, some seem to enhance it, or at least provide a window on how one might enhance such experience naturally once one has "broken through" an oppressive pattern. Among these drugs are the judicious use of marijuana, MDMA ("Ecstasy") and certain psychedelics. Controlled quantities of these drugs are already being used to successfully treat people with chronic pain, muscle disorders, post-traumatic stress and chronic depression. Despite these artificial enhancements of our capacity to experience awe, we should not forget that there are many natural chemicals in our bodies, such as those associated with awe directly, that are more powerful than we generally conceive and that may also be more ultimately rewarding. The challenge is to learn to tap these natural elements and prime their potential for expanded application to our lives. Depth therapy, meditation, impassioned artistry and certainly love can all be staging grounds for the arousal of such chemicals, and whatever other ingredients go to make up our unfathomable experiences of living.

Theodore Roszak summarized the problem well back in the heyday of the 60s counterculture. Psychedelic drugs, and the drug culture in general, he suggested, played an important role in young people's rejection of the technocratic society. "Yet," he goes on, it is the "frantic search for the pharmacological panacea which tends to distract many of [them] from all that is most valuable in their rebellion, and which threatens to destroy their most promising sensibilities." Among these sensibilities, he elaborates, is the natural "integrity of our organisms," and a "[good] deal of hard growing."[76]

- **The capacity to refuse high tech.** It is imperative to have the capacity to refuse technology that one does not desire. Wherever there are rules or laws about the use of technology, short of an emergency situation, it is critical to have "opt out" alternatives lest people become slaves to their machines or those promoting machines. These "opt outs" allow people to

---

[76] The quotes respectively are from T. Roszak's *The Making of a Counter Culture* (New York: Anchor Books, 1969, pp. 156 and 177).

unhook from their tech addictions, or from regulations they find oppressive, such as requirements for mental health professionals to drug people when more natural and equally effective alternatives are both desired and available; or when people would rather live with their physical disability than be pressured to accept a treatment that is onerous to them.

- **The capacity to take a meta-perspective on the corporate manipulation of high tech.** The awareness of product "branding" and the use of technology to promote that branding is a critical step toward fuller personal presence and the potential for an awe-based life. To the extent that people become unwitting pawns in a game of corporate definitions of fashion, power, beauty, intelligence and moral conduct, such people turn robotic. For example, if a computer company puts out a video game that glorifies killing so that it can make lavish profits on teenage boys, and the boys who consume such videos have no knowledge about that particular computer company's motives, then those boys become machine-like tools for the larger "machine" that seduces them. If hordes of shoppers purchase "ghetto" style clothing to vicariously experience "freedom"—and they forfeit tangible freedom as a result, then they risk becoming servants to manipulators.

These scenarios, and many like them, are precisely why present-centered, awe-based childrearing and exposure to arts and humanities are so critical; for they bring the meta-perspective that can help people understand how and why they are being molded, and what alternatives might exist to build a better world.

Consider, as a further example, the tech industry itself. What if the "best and the brightest" in that industry focused even more on planetary sustainability, social justice, cultural understanding, art, beauty, and personal well-being; and less on products such as: "A service that delivers your beer right to your door. An app that analyzes the quality of your French kissing. A "smart" button and zipper that alerts you if your fly is down. An app with speaker that plays music from within a mother's vaginal walls to her unborn baby.

A sensor placed in your child's diaper that sends you an alert when the diaper needs changing... A refrigerator advertised as "the Family Hub" that promises to act as a personal assistant, message board, stereo and photo album.

An app to locate rentable driveways for parking. An app to locate rentable yachts..."[77] You get the idea, and many more of us need to if there is to be a major shift in tech consciousness.

- **The capacity to reverse mechanical changes.** Whatever is done to mechanically transform human functioning must have a built-in reversibility option. Hence, if computer chips replace neurons, then there should be precautions taken for the potential of neurons to supplant the computer chips should those chips prove dissatisfactory. The same goes for any particularly mind-altering mechanical change.

The issue here is one of choice. Human beings must have the capacity to both assess and change their actions on the basis of evolving experience.

- **The need for technology that does not harm human beings.** The basis for this recommendation is to ensure that whatever technology is developed, it must be programmed not to harm people. Also known as fiction writer Isaac Asimov's First Law of Robotics, this recommendation could not be more timely. While the recommendation may not protect us from unintended consequences (can anything?), it would at least have the advantage of pressing us to think as critically and sensitively as possible whenever new technology is considered. Moreover, this First Law is precisely a basis for the convening of bio-ethics and experiential democracy committees described earlier. I think most people would want to know that whenever a technology is conceived which could substantially impact life, that technology will be scrutinized from all possible angles— physically, intellectually and spiritually.
- **Apply "lenses of awe" to life, and that includes our "life" with machines.** As an exercise in maintaining awe in the face of mechanical routine, the so-called lenses of awe, which are distillations of frameworks utilized by interviewees in my book *Awakening to Awe: Personal Stories of Profound Transformation,* may be notable. Each of the following lenses can help to deepen

---

[77] The quote listing amoral developments of technology is from Allison Arieff's "Solving All the Wrong Problems." *The New York Times* Sunday Review, July 9, 2016.

the experience of a particularly captivating film, for example, or of a virtual reality device, or even of a high-tech medical procedure. Again, the issue isn't so much what device is used, as *how* it is used and appropriated in one's life. Here are the metaphorical "lenses" that can be "tried on" as part of a lifelong experiment:

The Lens of Transience

This lens enables one to attune to the passing nature of time and the fragility of life. The more we sensitize to transience, the more we can appreciate the preciousness of the moment and the mysterious background within which the moment is formed. I often peer through this lens when I'm witnessing my son at play, or my family at a meal, but I can also experience it while walking in a particularly striking building, or driving on a mesmerizing bridge. Virtually any engagement can be perceived through this lens, because virtually any engagement can be understood in its fleeting and enigmatic character; its poignant character. It's not a far stretch, for example, to shift from the deeply moving observation of a loved one—or a beloved moment—to the deeply moving speculation about the rise and fall of creation itself. We're all a part of this drama, hurtling through the darkness, vanishing with the voids.

The Lens of Unknowing

Unlike transience, which focuses chiefly on time, the unknown extends to all dimensions—time, space, mind and heart. Unknowing eclipses all and tantalizes us with the source of all. It is the "worm at the core" but also the dazzle, grace and hope at the core. Although the unknown may be the greatest factor in the kindling of fear, as Rod Serling, the creator of *The Twilight Zone* intimated, it also may be the greatest factor in the fostering of fascination. Consider for example the role of unknowing in film, literature and fine art. How mesmerized we are by suspense thrillers, tales of adventure and enigmatic characters. How we stammer before sculptures, paintings and hymnals. Indeed, the whole of our natural and even manufactured world can be a wonder, riddled with puzzlements, both large and small. Scientists such as Einstein stood rapt before this spectacle, and were filled with exhilarating curiosity. But so do—and can—many of us, the moment we stop to reflect.

The Lens of Surprise

A chief aspect of unknowing is surprise. To the extent one can open to surprise, one can also enable spontaneity, novelty and reform—and certainly our technologies, such as the world-wide web, selective drug experiences, virtual reality and the like can aid in this receptivity. Being open to surprise also means being open to the flash of insight from one's memories, dreams and imaginings. It is a link to the unpredictable, like seeing the world, at least for moments, like a child. It is "big mind" in Zen Buddhist literature. For a child, each day is a blank canvas holding untold secrets and delights. It is a waiting paintbrush, a captivating story and a dazzling space ship. To the extent that we can approach these sensibilities and seize upon the "blank canvas" of our day, we can lift ourselves, even partially, out of our entrenched lives. We can "get out of our way" and greet the unexpected along our path; and we can breathe a little freer, a little fuller, wherever we are.

The Lens of Vastness

Here too we meet the cosmological, albeit in its most prodigious dimensions. The lens of vastness opens out in infinite directions. The moment I walk outdoors, for example, I engage it. I perceive it in the distances and horizons, in parks, and in planetariums, in the chemical make-up of matter, and amid the diversity of species. I connect with it while driving through urban sprawl and while peering into ocean sunsets. But beyond these physical settings, vastness embraces all that we perceive and intuit: it is the grand sweep of nature, the grand sweep of our lives.

The Lens of Intricacy

If the lens of vastness orients us to the macro and grand, the lens of intricacy situates us in the micro and hidden. For example, the lens of intricacy is what captivates many of us about meditation and psychotherapy. The themes that can come up can range from dizzying dreads to dazzling desires, and from meandering fantasies to timely practicalities. But the overarching effect is that the more one is informed by such engagements, the greater one's potential for a full and diversified life—a life of depth but also vibrancy. This sensibility can be illustrated by the time that one takes with both people and things. It can be seen in one's attentiveness to one's friends, loved ones, or acquaintances; in one's sensitivity to art, beauty and nature. When is the last time, for example, that you have attended to the markings on a leaf, or the brusqueness of an autumn wind, or the tenderness of a lover's skin? When have you stood in amazement at the intricacies of genetic testing such as that of "23andMe", the revelations of paleontology and the details of our knowledge about human physiology? How much time do you devote to digging beyond the requirements of a work assignment, or exploring alternative thoughts, philosophies, or lifestyles? These and so much more are the potentialities inherent as the lenses of intricacy are polished.

The Lens of Sentiment

The experiences of emotion and of being profoundly moved are the key features of this lens. Sentiment offers us a deepened sensibility, a refined feeling, toward both people and things; life and art. The question for this lens is to what extent can we "drop in" to it as exemplified by our responses to love and to loss, to beauty and to repulsion, or to any momentary encounter. How and in what ways can we linger over those sensibilities, take them in, and allow them to shake us to our core? For example, to what extent can we stand before beauty and allow our breath to be taken away? Can we permit this on our walk outside on a spring day; or in the face of a ravishing woman or man; or how about in the presence of a haunting melody? But how will sentiment bond with our increasingly mechanical world? Can we immerse in it through the resounding melodies in ear buds, or the "responsive" new robots in Japan that are working in gardens and helping the elderly in nursing homes? The effects of these human-robotic relationships are just beginning to emerge, and some level of sentiment—or what in the psychological literature might be called "bonding"—does indeed appear to be part of the equation.[78] The issue of its quality however is still very much in question, but what is less in doubt is that the more that sentiment becomes ingrained in one's life, in one's way of being in life, the more it is likely to enhance our experience of many relationships including those that are non-human,

---

[78] For a discussion of the "bonding" between Japanese elders and their robot caretakers, again see A. Massui's "Development of Care Robots Growing in Aging Japan." *The Japan Times,* January 27, 2016. Retrieved January 31st 2017 at http://www.japantimes.co.jp/news/2016/01/27/national/social-issues/development-care-robots-growing-aging-japan/#.WJGIxBHujm0.

and even non-organic.

The Lens of Solitude

This is one of the essential yet least celebrated lenses for awe. It may also be a prerequisite for the other lenses. To be sure, solitude is a state of aloneness; but it is also, as many in *Awakening to Awe* have testified, a state of aliveness, attentiveness and absorption. Solitude can be isolating, but it is not generally alienating. To the contrary, it is frequently renewing, deepening and strengthening. In this era of cell phones and instant messaging, solitude can clear a space for what really matters in one's life and for how to pursue what really matters. By encouraging us to step back, take a breath, and stay acutely present, solitude opens the way to multiple expressions of awe, both naturalistic and technical.

In sum, one can see the foundational value of solitude for virtually any relationship, be that with oneself, others, or with the world. To the degree that one can stay present and coexist with oneself, one is in a much improved position to stay present and coexist with all that surrounds one, such as life's transience, mystery, surprise, vastness, intricacy, poignancy, and in short, awe.

Final Thoughts

The robotic age has the potential to be an *awe-inspiring* dawn or a dehumanizing nightmare. The choice is ours.

The development of machinery such as driverless cars could free up space for people to speak to each other during commute hours; or such cars could become self-enclosed bubbles for self-enclosed riders.

The virtual reality machine, like the aforementioned "Oculus Rift," may become an exhilarating tool. It may be used to explore distant lands or fantastic visions, seascapes or ventures through space. Or, it could become a life-sucking obsession, a prison that precludes living breathing people, raw engagements with nature and active explorations of the imagination.

The neural chip could open up untold avenues of knowledge, precious stores of information and dazzling displays of physical and mental power. But it could also foster emotional blindness, constricted sensitivities and soul-sapping indignities.

Hence, the question of whether we become sensitized or desensitized by our devices is a critical one. The answer will set the course for the quality of our lives for many decades, and even lifetimes, to come. Hopefully this book will give readers a clearer picture of the stakes involved as we transition to a machine-saturated world.

If there is one message that I would like to stress it is the following: Machines, at least for the foreseeable future, are binary modalities. They rely on stimulus (input) and response (output) with little or no capacity to pause, reflect and grapple with choice. Or if they do "grapple," it is within strict parameters, dependent on pre-set rules. Given this state of affairs, we need to be very conscious about how we interact with machines, and in particular, how we *internalize* them. We need to protect our capacity to grapple, pause, and reflect *between* stimulus and response.

My conclusion is that this grappling, starting with childrearing and the impressionable psyches of newborns, is crucial to our humanity. It is crucial to education, work, play, religion and governance; not to "engineer" society, but to "nourish" it. Without mystery, discovery and the risk of pain, no machine in the world can give us vitality, let alone *awe*. The most it can give us is entrancement, the performance of actions and the seductive illusion of power. Yet, it is time we take back the enduring power of humility, wonder and love.

And from there oversee our machines.

Acknowledgements

I wish to express my profound gratitude to the people who have intimately accompanied me along this journey; without their engagement, sensitivity and depth of inquiry, the venture would have been much the poorer. Among those notable are Kathleen Galvin, Bob Goodwin, Jeff Schneider, Benjamin Schneider, Jurate Raulinaitis, Irena Raulinaitis, Laura Siegal, Alvin Siegal, Bob Edelstein, Graham Jenkin, Steve Walsh, Ilene Serlin, Jeff Saperstein, Dennis Portnoy, Danny Brook, Louis Hoffman, Ed Mendelowitz, Jeff Bricker, Donald Cooper, Bob Kramer, Scott Gibbs, Fraser Pierson, and my colleagues Orah Krug, Nader Shabahangi, Troy Piwowarski, Sonja Saltman, and Doug Silberstein at the Existential-Humanistic Institute. I also wish to thank my colleagues at the University Professors Press for their care and diligence in the production of this revised volume. To those I may have overlooked, my sincere apologies, but know that I am grateful. Finally, I want to convey my appreciation to the existential and humanistic philosophical tradition; for it is this lineage above most, which has foreseen, forewarned and forearmed us, if we would but attend.

Index